Collins
LITTLE BOOKS

SCOTTISH
CASTLES

HarperCollins Publishers
Westerhill Road
Bishopbriggs
Glasgow
G64 2QT

First Edition 2017

Reprint 10 9 8 7 6 5 4 3

© HarperCollins Publishers 2017

ISBN 978-0-00-825111-6

www.collins.co.uk

A catalogue record for this
book is available from the
British Library

Author: Chris Tabraham

Typeset by
Davidson Publishing Solutions

Printed and bound in China by
RR Donnelley APS Co Ltd

Contents

An introduction to Scotland's castles and fortified houses

Scotland is a country as rich in castles and fortified houses as any other in Europe. They range in date from the twelfth to the seventeenth centuries, and in size and complexity from the great royal fortresses at Edinburgh and Stirling, to the fortified houses of humble bonnet lairds (distinct from nobles and lairds in that they worked the land themselves, alongside their servants). This book is your guide to some of these structures. Almost 140 castles and fortified houses are included, selected because they have something of interest surviving today, and also because they are publicly accessible.

The castle was introduced into Scotland in the early twelfth century by the sons of Malcolm III. Most were motte castles (or motte-and-bailey castles), built mainly of timber on raised mounds (mottes) of earth.

The thirteenth century was, without doubt, Scotland's golden age as far as castles go. Great stone enclosure castles (sometimes called curtain-walled castles because their imposing encircling walls were drawn around the castle complex like a curtain) were built across the land, both by the kings and by the major aristocratic families. These mighty barons had huge households, numbering in excess of 200 people, and required large castles to house them all. Castle Sween, built c.1200 by Sven the Red, founder of the MacSween clan, is the oldest stone castle standing in Scotland today, whilst Bothwell (de Moray family), Caerlaverock (de Maxwell family), and Duart (MacLean family) are just as awesome today as they were way back then.

Those baronial families not quite so high up the social ladder built castles reflecting their less exalted status. We call these hall castles, because the focus of their castle life was centred on the feasting hall, generally located on the first floor above a storage undercroft. Few survive intact today – the best is Morton – but good examples can be found incorporated into later tower houses (e.g. Lochranza).

The Wars of Independence with England (1296–1356) had a profound effect on the political landscape of Scotland, as old baronial families disappeared, e.g. Balliol and Comyn, and new ones took their place, e.g. Campbell and Douglas. A new form of castle also appeared, centred on a lofty stone tower house; hence the tower-house castle. These could be five storeys high and more – Threave, one of the first, is equivalent in height to a ten-storey block of flats. The lofty tower was not a new concept – the oldest stone castle in Scotland, Cubbie Roo's Castle, built by a Viking jarl (chieftain) c.1145, was a modest tower – but the Scottish tower house that emerged after the Wars of Independence completely dominated the surrounding castle buildings, and functioned more truly as a private family home.

These early tower houses had massively thick walls and were usually rectangular on plan, e.g. Drum. Orchardton was the only circular tower house. During the fifteenth century, the walls got thinner and grew extensions (called jambs), generally to house the stair. Most castles had one jamb, e.g. Neidpath; hence the L-plan. A few had two, e.g. Borthwick, whilst Crookston and Hermitage, uniquely, had four.

There is a select group of royal residences dating from the reigns of the first five Jameses (1406–1542) that are called palaces. They are more like elegant manor houses, not in the least defensible; even the great bulwark added to Linlithgow Palace by James IV c.1500, was all show. Their existence reminds us too that there were many smaller manor houses dotted about the country, built mostly of wood, that were likewise not defensive – even their water-filled moats were intended only to keep out wolves and other wild beasts! (None of these moated sites is included in this book, as scarcely anything can be seen above ground today.)

Meanwhile, most noblemen continued their love affair with the tower-house castle. Through the sixteenth century and well into the seventeenth century, many hundreds were built the length and breadth of the land (which is why they dominate the book). They came in all shapes and sizes – square ones, rectangular ones, some with one jamb, some with two, three, or more, forming on plan various letters of the alphabet – Ls, Ts,

Zs, and Es, and variations of these. This proliferation is largely due to the Reformation of 1560, which resulted in church lands passing into private hands, mostly former monastery tenants. The tower houses they built were as much statements of wealth and power as the great castles and towers of an earlier age; the only difference was scale.

There are a handful of castles built around 1600 that did not have a tower house as their chief focus, but where the buildings were more equally ranged around a central courtyard; hence the term courtyard castle. Whereas earlier castles with courtyards (e.g. Crichton) resulted from subsequent changes to the original scheme, these later courtyard castles were designed as such from the outset. They are rare, and not truly representative. They signal in effect the demise of the Scottish castle and fortified house, and point to a newer, more residential style of noble living.

The medieval castle was a product of military feudalism, whereby lords held their land from the Crown in return for providing military service – e.g. one mounted knight or six archers. By 1603, when James VI of Scotland became also James I of England, that was no longer the case. During the seventeenth century, castles became a thing of the past, and great country houses, often called castles but not in the least defensive, took their place, e.g. Drumlanrig, built c.1680.

Certain castles are hard to categorize. The Castle of Old Wick and Cubbie Roo's Castle, for example, are exceedingly rare examples of twelfth-century tower-house castles built on lands that were under Norwegian rule. Dumbarton and Roxburgh were later extensively altered as artillery forts.

Most of the castles featured in this book are generally open to visitors (for example tourist attraction or hotel) and this is shown in the description for each castle by a green square. ■ However, there are a handful which are normally best viewed from outside (may be privately owned) and this is depicted by an orange square. ■

Where the property has notable gardens or grounds, this is also shown with the following symbol ❋.

The inclusion of a castle or fortified house in the book does not imply a right of access. The access categories are intended only as a general guide to visitor access. Castles managed by Historic Environment Scotland (formerly Historic Scotland), shown with the following symbol 🏛 and the National Trust for Scotland, shown with this symbol ♛ are generally open to visitors throughout the year. Tourist attraction opening and closing times, and other details, often change. It is always advisable to check with the attraction in advance. Telephone numbers and websites, where available, are listed in the property description.

Aberdour Castle

Easter Aberdour, Burntisland, Fife
01383 860519 | www.historicenvironment.scot

HALL CASTLE / TOWER-HOUSE CASTLE

A fine tower-house castle of the Douglas Earls of Morton, begun in the fourteenth century but thereafter greatly altered and extended. Much of the surviving ruin dates from the time of James Douglas, the 4th Earl, who as Regent Morton wielded great power in the 1570s until his execution in 1581 for his alleged part in the murder of Lord Darnley, Mary Queen of Scots's second husband. He was largely responsible for the fine terraced gardens here on the south side. Morton's title deeds refer to the 'castle, fortalice, manor, mills, fishery, township, woods, parks, gardens, orchards, doocots and warrens', a perfect description of a castle in James VI's Scotland. Almost lost in the ruins are the remains of one of Scotland's oldest masonry castle structures – a tower-keep built in the twelfth century by the de Mortimers, Norman incomers from England. The adjacent parish church of St Fillans was their handiwork too. By 1725 the crumbling castle had been abandoned by the Douglases in favour of a new mansion nearby, Cuttlehill (now Aberdour House).

Alloa Tower

Alloa, Clackmananshire, central Scotland
01259 211701 | www.nts.org.uk

TOWER-HOUSE CASTLE

The Erskines, Earls of Mar, were among the great Scottish aristocratic families, and Alloa Tower was one of their chief seats. David II granted the estate to his chamberlain, Sir Robert Erskine, in 1368. The great rectangular tower was probably built a century later. Four storeys and a garret high, it is topped by a crenellated (notched) parapet, with open 'rounds' at each corner. It was much altered by his descendants, particularly internally, and added to externally. There was once a large courtyard with ancillary buildings ranged around it; the triangle-shaped creases visible on this south side indicate where some of their roofs once were. By far the finest feature externally was an elaborate designed landscape, added by the 6th Earl c.1700. He fled into exile in 1716, following his failed attempt to seat James VIII & III on the throne of Great Britain. A fire in 1800 led to wholesale demolition, but the tower itself survived, not as a residence but as a feature of antiquarian interest amid the fast-expanding burgh of Alloa.

Arbuthnott House

Arbuthnott, Inverbervie, Aberdeenshire
01561 320417 | www.arbuthnott.co.uk

TOWER-HOUSE CASTLE

Arbuthnott has been the home of the Arbuthnotts since
Duncan 'de Aberbuthnot' built the first castle c.1200.
Fragments of it are entombed in the present building.
What stands today began as a hall house built c.1420
by Hugh, the 9th laird, then extended by Robert, the
12th laird, c.1475–90, further tinkered with by Andrew,
15th laird, in 1588, then gutted and modernized by
Robert, 20th laird, in the 1680s. What we see at this
entrance front today was largely created by John, 22nd
laird, in the 1750s, to provide symmetry to a group of
disconnected buildings.

Argyll's Lodging

Stirling
01786 450000 | www.historicenvironment.scot

COURTYARD CASTLE

Scotland's finest seventeenth-century town house.
A modest burgess's house until 1629, when Sir William
Alexander, 1st Earl of Stirling, purchased it. In the hope
of welcoming Charles I here during his coronation visit,
the Earl transformed it, adding lavish exteriors and
installing luxurious apartments within. Alas, he died
insolvent in 1640. Archibald Campbell, 9th Earl of Argyll,
purchased it in 1668 and extended it to serve as his
Lowland residence – hence its name.

Armadale Castle

Armadale, Sleat, Isle of Skye
01471 844305 | www.clandonald.com

CASTELLATED MANSION

Set amid the wooded landscape of Sleat, on the west side of the Isle of Skye, lies Armadale. It is not a real castle, rather a large country mansion – or was. Beginning in the late eighteenth century as a modest, two-storey house, it was transformed into a 'battlemented toy fort' by the architect, James Gillespie Graham, at the behest of the 1st Lord Macdonald of Sleat. His illustrious forebears had previously resided further north, near Uig, firstly at fifteenth-century Duntulm Castle before relocating to Monkstadt House in the 1730s. They remained at Armadale for a little over a century, enlarging it in the 1850s and adding a fine walled garden, before moving once more, this time to Ostaig. Their castellated home at Armadale burned down shortly thereafter, and little remains standing today. One remaining feature is the Imperial Stair with its Gothic-balustered landing (pictured). The nearby stables now house the Museum of the Isles and nature trails thread through the remnants of the walled garden and into the woods beyond.

Auchindoun Castle

Auchindoun, Dufftown, Moray
01667 460232 | www.historicenvironment.scot

TOWER-HOUSE CASTLE

Commanding the crest of a hill in lonely Glen Fiddich, beside the old hill road over the mountains to Strathdon. Who built this L-plan, four-storey tower house within its perimeter wall is a mystery. The finger of suspicion points to the shadowy figure of Thomas Cochrane, a favourite of James III (1460–88), who is reputed to have designed a number of buildings for his sovereign, for which he received the Earldom of Mar. Auchindoun's tower may look bleak and uninviting in its present ruined state, but its fine stone-ribbed vault over the first-floor hall indicates a building of no little sophistication. Cochrane soon fell from grace and was murdered by his fellow nobles at Lauder, in Berwickshire, in 1482. His Grampian stronghold passed first to the Ogilvies, then to Adam Gordon in 1567. The Gordons were often feuding with the Forbeses, over that hill road in Strathdon. Adam Gordon's chief claim to fame was to murder all the Forbeses sheltering in Corgarff Castle – an outrage made famous in the ballad 'Edom o Gordon'.

Balhousie Castle

Perth
01738 638152 | www.theblackwatch.co.uk

CASTELLATED MANSION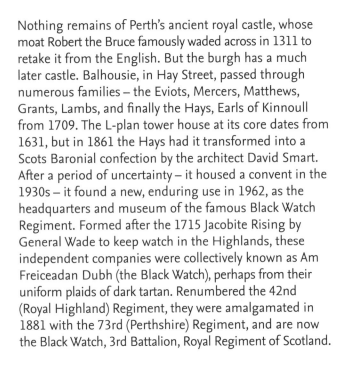

Nothing remains of Perth's ancient royal castle, whose moat Robert the Bruce famously waded across in 1311 to retake it from the English. But the burgh has a much later castle. Balhousie, in Hay Street, passed through numerous families – the Eviots, Mercers, Matthews, Grants, Lambs, and finally the Hays, Earls of Kinnoull from 1709. The L-plan tower house at its core dates from 1631, but in 1861 the Hays had it transformed into a Scots Baronial confection by the architect David Smart. After a period of uncertainty – it housed a convent in the 1930s – it found a new, enduring use in 1962, as the headquarters and museum of the famous Black Watch Regiment. Formed after the 1715 Jacobite Rising by General Wade to keep watch in the Highlands, these independent companies were collectively known as Am Freiceadan Dubh (the Black Watch), perhaps from their uniform plaids of dark tartan. Renumbered the 42nd (Royal Highland) Regiment, they were amalgamated in 1881 with the 73rd (Perthshire) Regiment, and are now the Black Watch, 3rd Battalion, Royal Regiment of Scotland.

Ballindalloch Castle

Banffshire, between Grantown-on-Spey and Aberlour
01807 500205 | www.ballindallochcastle.co.uk

TOWER-HOUSE CASTLE

Majestically sited where the rivers Avon and Spey meet, Ballindalloch is a handsome pile with a history reaching back to 1546, when John Grant built the first castle. This had been a fine tower house built on the Z-plan, with round towers projecting from opposing corners. The impressive stair tower housing the entrance rose a storey higher, and was topped by a square belvedere, added in 1602 by Patrick, 4th laird, and his wife, Helen Ogilvie, to provide them with fine views over their estate. Mercifully, their castle came through the national wars and the family's feuds with the neighbouring Gordons in the seventeenth century relatively unscathed, and two lower wings were added in the eighteenth century. However, the present castle's impressive appearance is down to its sensitive remodelling into an elegant, and comfortable, country house in 1847–50 for John Macpherson-Grant by the architects Mackenzie & Matthews. They gave the exterior that Scots Baronial look so beloved by the Victorians, and completely redesigned the interior in a consciously antiquarian style. The Macpherson-Grants remain there today.

Balloch Castle

Loch Lomond, Alexandria, West Dunbartonshire
01389 752977 | www.visitscotland.com

CASTELLATED MANSION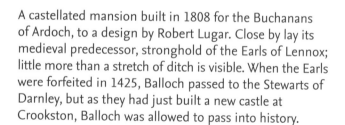

A castellated mansion built in 1808 for the Buchanans of Ardoch, to a design by Robert Lugar. Close by lay its medieval predecessor, stronghold of the Earls of Lennox; little more than a stretch of ditch is visible. When the Earls were forfeited in 1425, Balloch passed to the Stewarts of Darnley, but as they had just built a new castle at Crookston, Balloch was allowed to pass into history.

Balmoral Castle

Royal Deeside, Aberdeenshire,
between Ballater and Braemar
01339 742534 | www.balmoralcastle.com

CASTELLATED MANSION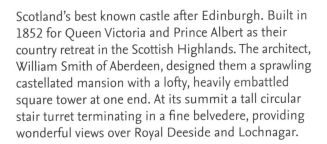

Scotland's best known castle after Edinburgh. Built in
1852 for Queen Victoria and Prince Albert as their
country retreat in the Scottish Highlands. The architect,
William Smith of Aberdeen, designed them a sprawling
castellated mansion with a lofty, heavily embattled
square tower at one end. At its summit a tall circular
stair turret terminating in a fine belvedere, providing
wonderful views over Royal Deeside and Lochnagar.

Balvenie Castle

near Dufftown, Moray
01340 820121 | www.historicenvironment.scot

ENCLOSURE CASTLE

Three of Scotland's greatest medieval noble dynasties ruled from Balvenie (or Mortlach as it was originally named). The massive, almost featureless, thirteenth-century curtain wall (left) was built by the 'Black Comyns', Earls of Buchan. They and their 'Red Comyn' cousins then ruled northern Scotland from the Moray Firth to the Atlantic Ocean until their downfall fighting Robert the Bruce in 1308. The victorious king gifted their forfeited castle to his right-hand man, 'the Good Sir James' of Douglas, and the Black Douglases held it for over 100 years, building new internal ranges. They too were brought down, by James II in 1455, and he likewise entrusted the stronghold to a loyal kinsman, John Stewart, Earl of Atholl. His descendant, the 4th Earl, transformed the awesome stronghold into an elegant Renaissance residence, replacing much of the entrance front with the noble Atholl Lodging during Mary Queen of Scots's reign; Queen Mary visited in 1562. The castle's unique double-leafed iron yett (cross-barred gate) still hangs inside the round-arched entrance gate.

Barcaldine Castle

Benderloch, near Oban
01631 720598 | www.barcaldinecastle.co.uk

TOWER-HOUSE CASTLE

An impressive tower-house castle in Benderloch, for a long time the property of the Campbells. Its builder was Sir Duncan Campbell, 7th laird of Glenorchy, in 1601–9. Quite why he needed yet another castle when he already had five – Achallader, Balloch (now Taymouth), Edinample, Kilchurn, and Loch Dochart – is not clear; his by-name, though, was 'Black Duncan of the Castles'. His latest residence was an L-plan tower, three floors and a garret high, with a circular stair tower tucked into the angle. The tower walls are pierced by gunholes, and the chunky iron yett (cross-barred gate) behind the front door is there yet. The Campbells of Barcaldine were clearly anticipating trouble. One of Duncan's more notorious descendants was Sir John Cambell of Barcaldine, half-brother of Sir Colin Campbell of Glenure, alias 'the Red Fox'. The latter was shot and killed in 1752, a story that Robert Louis Stevenson made famous in his novel *Kidnapped*. Sir John had James Stewart tried and hanged for the crime, with the help of a jury almost entirely composed of Campbells!

Bass of Inverurie

Inverurie, Aberdeenshire
www.undiscoveredscotland.co.uk

MOTTE CASTLE

The first castles in Scotland were mostly motte-and-baileys, constructed of earth and timber. They were introduced in the 12th century by incomers from northern France and Flanders, who had crossed the English Channel into England with William the Conqueror. They came to Scotland not as conquerors, though, but at the behest of her kings – David I (1124-53) and his grandsons, Malcolm IV (1153-65) and William 'the Lion' (1165-1214). One of the best motte-and-baileys was built by Malcolm and William's young brother, David, Earl of Huntingdon and Lord of Garioch. His English seat was Fotheringhay, where Mary Queen of Scots was executed in 1587. His seat in Aberdeenshire was the Bass of Inverurie. Built c.1180 beside where the rivers Urie and Don intertwine, the large motte, or mound (left), held his tower-residence, whilst the bailey, known as the Little Bass (right), housed his feasting hall, chapel, stables and other ancillary buildings. Robert the Bruce used the Bass as his base in 1308 in his battle to overcome his over-mighty subjects, the Comyn Earls of Buchan.

Birsay, Earl's Palace

Birsay, north end of Mainland, Orkney
01856 721205 | www.historicenvironment.scot

COURTYARD CASTLE

Begun by Robert Stewart, Earl of Orkney, in the 1570s,
and completed by his son Patrick. Their principal country
seat, it was a fine residence. No tower-house castle this,
but four ranges around a central courtyard, with towers
projecting from the corners. The long gallery on an
upper floor was 'prettily decored'. Neither father nor son
was much liked by the Orcadians, and 'Black Patie' was
executed in 1615.

Blackness Castle

Blackness, near Bo'ness and Linlithgow
01506 834807 | www.historicenvironment.scot

TOWER-HOUSE CASTLE

The 'ship that never sailed'. Built for the powerful
Crichtons in the 1440s, it was seized by James II and
upscaled into a formidable artillery fortification, with
massively-thick walls and huge wide-mouthed gunholes.
A state prison until 1707, with inmates including
Cardinal Beaton and many Covenanters. Converted into
an ammunition depot in the 1870s, serving the island
defences in the Forth and the naval dockyard across the
water at Rosyth.

Blair Castle

Blair Atholl, Pitlochry, Perthshire
01796 481207 | www.blair-castle.co.uk

TOWER-HOUSE CASTLE ❋ ■

Ancestral seat of the Earls, Marquises, and finally Dukes
of Atholl. A brilliant-white battlemented Baronial castle,
majestically set within a mountained landscape. Although
substantially remodelled in the eighteenth and nineteenth
centuries, its oldest part, Cumming's (Comyn's) Tower, dates
back to the 1200s, when the powerful John Comyn, Lord
of Badenoch, held sway here. Sir James Stewart of Lorn
acquired the estate in 1439, and his descendants extended
the castle down the years. The 1st Earl of Atholl contributed
a three-storey block c.1530, and further extensions followed
in the early 1600s and the 1740s. The 7th Duke had the
exterior given the Baronial treatment c.1870, with the usual
panoply of crowstepped gables, pepperpot turrets, and
crenellations. Visited in turn by Edward III of England,
James V, and Mary Queen of Scots. The body of the Jacobite
general, Viscount 'Bonnie' Dundee, was brought here after
his pyrrhic victory over the army of William and Mary at
nearby Killiecrankie in 1690. The castle has the distinction
of being the last in Britain to be laid siege to – by 'Butcher'
Cumberland's government army en route to the battle of
Culloden in 1746. Robert Burns visited in 1787. The present
Duke of Atholl maintains the only private army in Europe.

Borthwick Castle

North Middleton, Gorebridge, Edinburgh
01875 820514 | www.borthwickcastle.com

TOWER-HOUSE CASTLE

Hidden away in a quiet Midlothian vale is one of Scotland's most impressive, complete, and unusual castles. Built by Sir William Borthwick, who acquired the lands from the Hays c.1430. Why he chose to build such a remarkable tower house isn't known. Unusually U-shaped on plan, it rises to over 30m, its walls crowned by an eye-catching corbelled-out machicolated parapet with open 'rounds' at each corner. Unlike most other contemporary towers, Borthwick had everything its lord and lady needed within – storage cellars and prison, hall and kitchen, chapel and private chambers – entered through a first-floor doorway. The hall was spacious, with a great fireplace at one end and minstrels' gallery; the kitchen was in an adjacent tower. The upper floors provided a chapel and an abundance of private chambers for Lord and Lady Borthwick, their family, household, and guests. Mary Queen of Scots and her third husband, James Hepburn, 4th Earl of Bothwell, stayed here in 1567. Lord and Lady Borthwick were laid to rest in their collegiate kirk nearby; their fine stone effigies still survive.

Bothwell Castle

Bothwell, Uddingston, South Lanarkshire
01698 816894 | www.historicenvironment.scot

ENCLOSURE CASTLE / TOWER-HOUSE CASTLE

Overlooking the River Clyde stands Scotland's largest
and finest thirteenth-century curtain-walled castle. Built
by William of Moray in the 1270s, it was much fought
over during the Wars of Independence (1296–1356).
The shattered castle was rebuilt by Countess Joanna of
Moray and Archibald 'the Grim', 3rd Earl of Douglas.
Their son, Archibald, added the great hall, chapel, and
the round tower (pictured), crowned with crenellations,
prior to his death in France in 1424.

Braemar Castle

Braemar, Ballater, Aberdeenshire
01339 741219 | www.braemarcastle.co.uk

TOWER-HOUSE CASTLE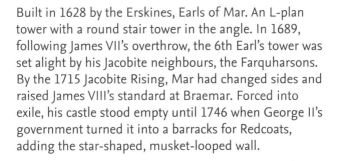

Built in 1628 by the Erskines, Earls of Mar. An L-plan tower with a round stair tower in the angle. In 1689, following James VII's overthrow, the 6th Earl's tower was set alight by his Jacobite neighbours, the Farquharsons. By the 1715 Jacobite Rising, Mar had changed sides and raised James VIII's standard at Braemar. Forced into exile, his castle stood empty until 1746 when George II's government turned it into a barracks for Redcoats, adding the star-shaped, musket-looped wall.

Brechin Castle

Brechin, Angus
01356 624566 | www.dalhousieestates.co.uk

CASTELLATED MANSION

Overlooking the River South Esk, in Brechin, is a large, three-storey mansion. Mostly built for James Maule, 4th Earl of Panmure, 1696–1711, but with remains of an earlier L-plan tower house lurking within. The east side (pictured) has eleven bays attractively faced in red sandstone, with round towers at either end and a slightly advanced centre. In the tympanum at the top is an eye-catching heraldic achievement displaying the arms of the Maules and the Hamiltons, for Lady Margaret, daughter of the Duke of Hamilton, who became the 4th Earl's wife. Although he was forfeited soon after completing his mansion, for his part in the 1715 Jacobite Rising, the family later returned to their lands and title. They and their successors, the Ramsays of Dalhousie, to whom it passed through marriage, further extended it, and encircled it with a fine landscaped park and walled garden. Nothing survives of the first castle here, made famous in 1296 when King John Balliol, 'Toom Tabard' (empty surcoat), was compelled to abdicate by Edward I of England, 'Hammer of the Scots'.

Brodick Castle

Brodick, Isle of Arran
01770 302202 | www.nts.org.uk

TOWER-HOUSE CASTLE

Impressively sited overlooking Brodick Bay, on Arran. The 'fairytale' castle was brought to its present form in the 1840s by the architect, James Gillespie Graham, to help the 10th Duke of Hamilton's son celebrate in fine style his marriage to Princess Marie of Baden, Napoleon III's cousin. It was Gillespie Graham's first experiment with Scots Baronial architecture, and what we see here at the west front is typical, with its corbelled-out crenellated parapets, pepperpot turrets, and crowstepped gables. The Hamiltons acquired much of Arran, including the castle, in the later 1400s, through marriage into the ruling Stewart dynasty. In the 1550s, James Hamilton, 2nd Earl of Arran, remodelled a stronghold begun in the 1200s by the Stewarts. Gillespie Graham did his utmost to retain what he could of these, without compromising the newly-weds' desire for a grand palace. Brodick has a bloody past – attacked by the Norsemen, English, Lords of the Isles, Campbells, and Cromwell's 'Roundheads'. Now a peaceful National Trust for Scotland property, it is surrounded by fine gardens and grounds, and overlooked by Goatfell, the highest peak on Arran.

Brodie Castle

near Forres, Moray
01309 641371 | www.nts.org.uk

TOWER-HOUSE CASTLE

Brodie Castle is well-named, for its Brodie owners have been lords here since the twelfth century. Nothing now dates from those far-off times. The present impressive building began as an L-plan tower house built c.1550 for the 11th Brodie of Brodie, to which the 12th Brodie added the tall tower (left) to create a more commodious Z-plan residence. The 15th Brodie added the wing behind (far left) c.1640, and the 22nd Brodie the twin-gabled block (right) and much else besides in 1825–8.

Broughty Castle

Broughty Ferry, Dundee
01382 436916 | www.historicenvironment.scot

TOWER-HOUSE CASTLE / OTHER

Broughty, 'strong point on the Tay', was built by Lord Gray c.1495 to help defend the coast from English warships. It failed to deliver. In 1547, after the Scots' defeat at Pinkie, it fell into English hands. A chance to redeem its reputation came in 1860–1, when the French were threatening invasion. The War Office turned the tower into a barracks and built a gun battery beside it. The French never showed. The only shots fired were a salute to mark Prince Albert's death in 1861.

Burleigh Castle

Milnathort, Kinross, near Perth
01786 450000 | www.historicenvironment.scot

TOWER-HOUSE CASTLE

Amid the lush Kinross-shire countryside stands the fortified residence built for the Balfours of Burleigh. Sir John Balfour had acquired the estate c.1445, and either he or his son built the three-storey and attic tower house (left) standing at one corner of a quadrangular courtyard. The tower's parapet is supported on continuous corbelling with open 'rounds' at three of the corners and a caphouse housing the spiral stair at the fourth. Of the courtyard buildings little remains but the west wall (centre) housing the entrance gate, and a projecting tower at the SW corner (right). This last is the chief delight of the place, with its oversailing rectangular top storey carried on corbelling above a circular ground floor. Decorative skew-putts on the roof gables declare that the structure was built in 1582 by Sir James Balfour of Pittendreich and his good lady, Margaret Balfour, heiress of Burleigh. What the stonework omits to tell us is that Sir James had been declared a traitor in 1579, and that the property had passed to his wife and son!

Caerlaverock Castle

Glencaple, near Dumfries
01387 770244 | www.historicenvironment.scot

ENCLOSURE CASTLE

Close beside the salt marshes of the Solway Firth, this is the site of two castles of the Maxwells, successively Lords, Marquises, and finally Earls of Nithsdale. The first modest hall-house castle, built c. 1220 in the nearby woods, was replaced by the present, formidable curtain-walled castle in the 1270s. Its triangular form is unique in the British Isles. A contemporary poem recording the great siege by Edward I of England, 'Hammer of the Scots', in 1300, tells that 'in shape it was like a shield'. The remains of two wooden bridges across its water-filled moat, found in the 1950s, were dated to c.1279 and c.1370. The first records the castle's building whilst the latter coincides with its reconstruction following the Wars of Independence with England (1296–1356). The fine battlemented wall-heads date from the early fifteenth century. The interior was subsequently graced by a splendid Renaissance mansion added by the 1st Earl of Nithsdale in the 1630s, shortly before the Covenanters besieged and captured the place, so ending Caerlaverock's distinguished history as the strongest castle on the Scottish West March.

Cardoness Castle

Gatehouse of Fleet, Castle Douglas, Kirkcudbrightshire
01557 814427 | www.historicenvironment.scot

TOWER-HOUSE CASTLE

Built by Gilbert McCulloch on acquiring the estate c.1460.
The rectangular, six-storey tower has few windows but
numerous gunholes. But this dour exterior masks a fine
interior, especially the hall on the first floor, with its
handsome fireplace and adjacent wall-cupboard. There is
evidence for an outer feasting hall. The McCullochs were
a wild bunch, frequently feuding with the neighbouring
Gordons. Godfrey, last of their line, was beheaded in
Edinburgh in 1697.

Carnasserie Castle

Kilmartin, near Lochgilphead, Argyll & Bute
0131 668 8600 | www.historicenvironment.scot

TOWER-HOUSE CASTLE

The residence not of a laird but a clergyman, Rev. John Carswell, who became Bishop of the Isles after the Reformation of 1560. His residence is among the most accomplished in Jacobean Scotland – a tall residential tower (right) and adjacent hall range (left) integrated into one building. Its innovative design was complemented by the quality of its architecture, with finely-carved features inside and out. Bishop Carswell translated John Knox's Book of Common Order here, the first book printed in Gaelic.

Carsluith Castle

near Creetown, Dumfries & Galloway
0131 668 8600 | www.historicenvironment.scot

TOWER-HOUSE CASTLE

An eye-catching, L-plan tower house beside the busy
A75, containing two vaulted cellars, a roomy first-floor
hall and private chambers over, reached by a spiral
stair in the wing. The carved panel over the entrance
(now illegible) proclaimed that it was built in 1568 by
the Brouns. But their tower isn't what it seems. The stair
tower sits awkwardly, its top storey covering an old
window. What the Brouns did in 1568 was not build
a new tower but add a stair tower to an existing
rectangle, thereby increasing the accommodation
and improving circulation.

Castle Campbell

Dollar, Clackmananshire, central Scotland
01259 742408 | www.historicenvironment.scot

TOWER-HOUSE CASTLE

Built in the early fifteenth century and originally known as Castle Gloom. In the 1480s, it was rebuilt and renamed Castle Campbell by the Campbell Earls of Argyll as their Lowland seat, close to Stirling Castle. Mary Queen of Scots visited in 1563, residing not in the original lofty tower (right) but in the more spacious palace overlooking the terraced garden. Cromwell's Roundheads torched the place in the 1650s, forcing the Earls to relocate to Argyll's Lodging, Stirling. The views from the tower are stunning.

Castle Fraser

Kemnay, near Inverurie, Aberdeenshire
01330 833463 | www.nts.org.uk

TOWER-HOUSE CASTLE 👹 ❋ ▪

This accomplished Z-plan tower-house castle has been described as 'one of the great masterpieces of the Scottish Renaissance'. Formerly known as the House of Muchall-in-Mar, it was begun soon after Thomas Fraser acquired the barony in 1454. The relatively plain four-storey tower (centre left) dates from that time. Not that there is much evidence here on the outside, for by 1576 Michael Fraser had extended it to the west (left) and added two towers – one square and the other round – to create an expansive Z-plan residence, the largest in NE Scotland. As if that wasn't sufficient, son Andrew heightened the entire structure in the 1630s, creating the eye-catching Round Tower, rising through seven storeys and culminating in an impressive balustraded flat roof with a delicate 'stair-tourelle' in the angle between tower and main block. On completion in 1633, Andrew was made 1st Lord Fraser by Charles I, but it was only in the early 1700s that the residence was renamed Castle Fraser. Further additions behind this splendid south front, and alterations within, were made in the 1790s and c.1820–50. The interior is graced by some exemplary Regency-style work, and many Fraser family portraits.

Castle Menzies

Weem, near Aberfeldy, Perthshire
01887 820982 | www.castlemenzies.org

TOWER-HOUSE CASTLE

Impressive and picturesque in its landscape setting.
Built by James Menzies and his wife Barbara Stewart,
daughter of the 3rd Earl of Atholl, in the 1570s. It originally
took the form of a Z-plan tower house (right), with a
large central block, four storeys high, to which two square
towers were added at opposing corners, of similar height
but each with an extra floor. Fancy pedimented dormer
windows rose from the eaves, chunky rounded turrets
topped the corners, and steep crowstepped gables
climbed to the chimney stacks at its summit. As if this
wasn't big, or grand, enough, subsequent Menzies
owners added to it. An eighteenth-century wing has
long been demolished, but the large Baronial wing (left),
designed by the architect, William Burn, for Sir Neil,
6th Baronet, and added in the early 1840s, remains.
The castle has had its fair share of notable guests down
the years. Bonnie Prince Charlie stayed here a couple
of nights in 1746 on his way to the Battle of Culloden;
'Prince Charlie's Room' is in the SW tower (right).
The castle has served as the centre of the Clan Menzies
Society since 1957.

Castle of Mey

near John O' Groats, Caithness
01847 851473 | www.castleofmey.org.uk

TOWER-HOUSE CASTLE

Famous not for its medieval lords but for its recent lady
owner. Queen Elizabeth the Queen Mother holidayed
here every summer from 1952 until her death in 2002.
The original owners were the medieval bishops of
Caithness, but after the Reformation in 1560 the Sinclairs,
Earls of Caithness, took possession. They built the
three-storey Z-plan tower house at the heart of the
present complex. The residence has since undergone
several extensions and alterations, most notably by
William Burn c.1820.

Castle of Old Wick

near Wick, Caithness
01667 460232 | www.historicenvironment.scot

OTHER

The 'Old Man of Wick' can claim to be the oldest standing castle in Scotland. Not that it lay in Scotland when built. Twelfth-century Caithness was under Norwegian rule, and its likely builder, Earl Harald Maddadson, was Earl of Orkney and Caithness. The 'Old Man' was probably built as his mainland residence. Entered at an upper level, it has few openings through its thick walls and the only fireplace, on an upper floor, was a 'hingin lum' not an integral chimney flue.

Castle Sween

eastern shore of Loch Sween, near Achnamara, Argyll
0131 668 8600 | www.historicenvironment.scot

ENCLOSURE CASTLE / TOWER-HOUSE CASTLE

Perched on a ridge overlooking Loch Sween, Caisteal Suibhne has the distinction of being the oldest standing castle in Scotland that can be dated with confidence – to the later twelfth century. Its builder was Suibhne (Sven) 'the Red', Lord of Knapdale, founder of Clan MacSween. His very name proclaims that Norse blood coursed through his veins. His castle is well-nigh unique – a quadrangular curtain-wall 8m high to its battlements, enclosing an area the size of two tennis courts, and entered through a round-arched doorway; a back gate led down to the loch-side. The twelfth-century date is confirmed by the shallow, broad buttresses clasping the outside walls. The MacSweens were ousted as Lords of Knapdale following the inconclusive battle of Largs between Hakon IV of Norway and Alexander II of Scotland in 1263. They were replaced by the Stewarts of Menteith. In a bid to reclaim his inheritance, John MacSween, c.1300, sailed a fleet of galleys into the loch but failed to retake the castle. The attempt prompted the Stewarts to build a three-storey tower overlooking the loch. An even larger tower (right) was added by the MacMillans, owners in the fifteenth century.

Cawdor Castle

Cawdor, near Nairn
01667 404401 | www.cawdorcastle.com

TOWER-HOUSE CASTLE ✳ ◼

One of the most romantic castles in Scotland, despite
having no link with Shakespeare's Thane of Cawdor in
Macbeth. Tradition places its origin in the late fourteenth
century, when Donald Calder, the 5th Thane, selected the
site by letting a donkey laden with gold roam around
until it stopped by a tree. In reality, the earliest fabric is a
tall, plain, four-storey tower at the heart of the complex,
built c.1454 for William, 6th Thane. It still retains a
massive iron yett (cross-barred gate), brought by the
6th Thane from nearby Lochindorb Castle during
demolition works ordered by James II. The Campbells of
Argyll acquired Cawdor in 1510 following the marriage of
the young heiress, Muriel Calder, to the 2nd Earl's son,
John Campbell of Muckairn. Thereafter, the medieval
castle was crowded around by an assortment of buildings,
most dating to the seventeenth century. The castle
interiors are graced by a magnificent collection of
family portraits, tapestries, fixtures, and furnishings,
whilst the splendid gardens include a seventeenth-
century walled garden and eighteenth-century flower
garden. The Campbells remain in residence to this day.

Claypotts Castle

near Broughty Ferry, Dundee
01786 450000 | www.historicenvironment.scot

TOWER-HOUSE CASTLE

One of Scotland's most attractive tower houses, built after the Reformation (1560) by John and Eufame Strachan. Formerly tenants of Lindores Abbey, the couple upscaled after 1560, building an unusual Z-plan tower. Its four storeys were innovatively laid out, with two stairs, not one, enabling them to have their private apartment in one tower and their household and guests in the other. The top floor, originally a gallery with balconies, gave fine views over the countryside.

Corgarff Castle

near Strathdon, Aberdeenshire
01975 651460 | www.historicenvironment.scot

TOWER-HOUSE CASTLE

A sixteenth-century tower house of the Forbeses,
dramatically sited in Strathdon. Famed in the ballad
'Edom o Gordon', recording the smoking out in 1571 of
Margaret Forbes and her household by Adam Gordon of
Auchindoun, in which all died. Bonnie Prince Charlie's
Jacobites occupied it prior to Culloden in 1746. After the
battle, George II's government gutted it to provide a
barracks for Redcoats patrolling Strathdon. They built
the star-shaped, musket-looped wall.

Craigievar Castle

near Alford, Aberdeenshire
01339 883635 | www.nts.org.uk

TOWER-HOUSE CASTLE 👹 ❀ ▪

Craigievar's pretty, pink-harled walls are an essay in Scottish Baronial architecture. Completed c.1626, the lofty L-plan tower rises six storeys high, modestly plain until the boldly carved corbel-course, above which a plethora of pepperpot turrets, crowstepped gables, and pedimented dormers grace the skyline. The whole achievement is brought to a crowning glory by a belvedere high over the entrance door, topped by a fine balustraded parapet, giving stunning views over the Aberdeenshire countryside. The interior is equally impressive, particularly the great hall on the first floor with its ornate plasterwork, including a huge display of the Royal Arms, among the finest in Britain. Strange then to discover that Craigievar was not created by some landed aristocrat but by a wealthy Aberdeen merchant and provost of that city, William Forbes, who made his fortune from his lucrative dealings with the Baltic states; whence his nickname 'Danzig Willie'. The tower is not entirely his, for when he bought it in 1610 from its impoverished owners, the Mortimers, they had already begun to build it; the great hall fireplace was their handiwork.

Craigmillar Castle

Edinburgh
0131 661 4445 | www.historicenvironment.scot

TOWER-HOUSE CASTLE

Situated in the southern suburbs of Edinburgh is one of the most extensive tower-house castles in Scotland, honeycombed with dark chambers and stairwells, interspersed with open courts and grass lawns. At its core is one of Scotland's oldest tower houses, built in the later fourteenth century by the Prestons, frequent provosts of Edinburgh. L-planned and three storeys high, with a capacious hall and adjacent court kitchen on the first floor and numerous unusual features, not least the turnpike stair that changes direction halfway up. The views from its wallheads are superb, particularly of Edinburgh's Old Town, Arthur's Seat, and the Firth of Forth. Over time, the Prestons developed Craigmillar into a sophisticated residence, with more comfortable ranges set within a fine courtyard wall, its projecting corner towers fitted with 'keyhole' gunloops. Beyond lay a designed landscape, including a fishpond formed into the letter P (for Preston), where the family and their guests could relax away from the intrigue of Edinburgh. Mary Queen of Scots sought solace here several times. The local place name Little France is said to have acquired its name from the queen's extensive household, which she brought from France to Scotland.

Craignethan Castle

Crossford, near Lanark, Lanarkshire
01555 860364 | www.historicenvironment.scot

TOWER-HOUSE CASTLE

The last private stronghold built in Scotland, and perhaps
the most unusual. Sir James Hamilton of Finnart built his
hideaway in the 1530s. At its core a massive rectangular
tower, unique in having more than one room at each
level. Around it a formidable artillery wall, including a
rare caponier (vaulted gun-chamber) in the great ditch.
Slighted after Mary Queen of Scots's downfall in 1568,
the ruin was bought by the Hays in 1665, who built the
modest house in the outer courtyard.

Crathes Castle

near Banchory, Aberdeenshire
01330 844525 | www.nts.org.uk

TOWER-HOUSE CASTLE

One of Scotland's finest castles. The massive tower
house took forever to build (1553–1596). Four storeys
high, its skyline is arrayed with corbelled-out turrets,
circular stair towers, and tall chimney stacks such as
were then becoming fashionable. The interiors are
equally stunning, the highlight being five painted
ceilings. Outside the tower is an eighteenth-century
walled garden. All this was the work of the Burnetts of
Leys, granted the lands by Robert the Bruce in 1323 and
with whom it remained until 1951.

Crichton Castle

near Gorebridge, Edinburgh
01875 320017 | www.historicenvironment.scot

TOWER-HOUSE CASTLE

Crichton is a hidden gem. Tucked out of sight on a terrace overlooking the River Tyne in Midlothian, this impressive tower-house castle served as a noble residence for two powerful dynasties for over 200 years. The Crichtons began it in the late fourteenth century when John de Crichton built the bulky tower house (right foreground) at a corner of a walled courtyard. His son William, 1st Lord Crichton, James II's Chancellor and one of the most powerful men in the land, greatly enlarged it, building an innovative great-hall block on the south side of the courtyard (left), where its tall, spacious windows could bathe the guests in sunlight. When the Crichtons fell from grace in 1488, their castle passed to the Hepburns, Earls of Bothwell. Mary Queen of Scots, who in 1566 married James Hepburn, the 4th Earl, attended a wedding here in 1562. In the 1580s, the 5th Earl added the castle's most extraordinary structure, a new north lodging with an attention-grabbing diamond-faceted facade; unique in Scotland, it would have looked more at home in Italy or Spain.

Crookston Castle

Glasgow
0141 883 9606 | www.historicenvironment.scot

TOWER-HOUSE CASTLE

Standing atop a prominent hill, and now surrounded by suburban Glasgow, Crookston was once a country seat of the Stewarts of Darnley. This junior branch of the High Stewards of Scotland duly climbed the aristocratic ladder when Robert, 7th Steward, became Robert II in 1371. By c.1400, Sir John Stewart of Darnley had built a fine castle; the date was confirmed in 1973 when a silver penny of Robert III was found in a foundation trench during excavations. His tower house was all but unique. Rather than the rectangular or L-plan favoured by his peers, his comprised a large, oblong central block to which four smaller towers were added, one at each corner. The two towers facing west towards the entrance have long gone, destroyed by bombardment in James IV's siege of 1489, which effectively ended Crookston's days as a noble residence. Sir John's great tower wasn't the first castle on the site. In the later twelfth century, Robert le Croc, a vassal of Walter, the 1st Steward, built a timber castle, now long gone, within a great ditch, which is still there – whence 'Croc's toun', or Crookston.

Crossraguel Abbey

Maybole, Ayrshire
01655 883113 | www.historicenvironment.scot

TOWER-HOUSE CASTLE

We normally associate castles with lords, but they also housed the senior clergy. A fine tower-house castle graces twelfth-century Crossraguel Abbey. In the early 1500s, William Kennedy became abbot and built a tower house for himself and his household near the cloister (far right), and an impressive gatehouse into the outer precinct (left). Three storeys and a garret high, the abbot had it provided with gunholes and battlements, and a round stair tower crowned by a watch chamber.

Cubbie Roo's Castle

Wyre, Orkney
01856 841815 | www.historicenvironment.scot

OTHER

Cubbie Roo may look modest, but it has the distinction
of being Scotland's oldest stone castle. The Orkneyinga
Saga relates that c.1145 Kolbein Hruga, a young man who
lived on Wyre, built a fine stone castle there – 'it was a
strong defence'. Only the basement exists today, its only
features two slit windows and a water tank in the bedrock.
The entrance must have been at an upper level. Close by,
Kolbein Hruga built a church, dedicated to St Mary.

Culcreuch Castle

Fintry, near Stirling
01360 860555 | www.culcreuch.com

TOWER-HOUSE CASTLE

Nestling in the lea of the pretty Fintry Hills, and set within acres of parkland. The original rectangular tower house (left) was built in the fifteenth century by the Galbraiths of Culcreuch. Standing three storeys and a garret high, and topped by a neat corbelled-out, crenellated (notched) parapet. Within was the standard tower house layout – vaulted service basement, first-floor hall, and private chambers above. The Galbraiths were among the rebels supporting the Earl of Lennox and Lord Lyle against the new king, James IV, in 1489. But whereas their lordships' castles at Crookston and Duchal were badly damaged by cannon-fire, Culcreuch came through unscathed. The Galbraiths finally got their 'come-uppence' in 1622 when debts compelled them to sell to the Setons and emigrate to Ireland. By the early 1700s the estate was in the hands of the Napier family. In 1721, according to a date stone, John Napier added the four-storey extension and north wing (right). One of the delights John Napier added within was the Chinese Bird Room, in the old tower, decorated with hand-painted Chinese wallpaper, thought to be the only example in Scotland.

Culzean Castle

near Maybole, Ayrshire
01655 884455 | www.nts.org.uk

CASTELLATED MANSION

A truly awe-inspiring Baronial mansion in Carrick, perched on a cliff overlooking the Firth of Clyde, and with hundreds of acres of gardens, grounds, and parkland laid out before it. Carrick was Kennedy country in the Middle Ages, but nothing remains now of their medieval stronghold, and only parts of the L-plan tower house they built here in the sixteenth century. What visitors see today is a magnificent castellated country house, designed by the famous Robert Adam and constructed 1777–92 for Thomas and David Kennedy, respectively 9th and 10th Earls of Cassilis. The splendid south entrance front (pictured) has tiers of pleasingly symmetrical windows set within a facade of warm sandstone. The frieze above the second tier of central windows is studded with carved lozenges displaying the Kennedy arms and emblems, leaving visitors in no doubt whose mansion they were entering. The house is equally stunning within, particularly the great Oval Staircase and the capacious Circular Room. President Dwight D. Eisenhower was given a 'grace-and-favour' flat here in recognition of his services to the United Kingdom during World War II.

Dalhousie Castle

Newtongrange, near Edinburgh
01875 820153 | www.dalhousiecastle.co.uk

TOWER-HOUSE CASTLE

A residence of the Ramsays from the thirteenth to the early twentieth century. In 1633, Sir William Ramsay was made Earl of Dalhousie by Charles I, and celebrated by remodelling and extending his ancestral seat. This is what we mostly see today. But entombed within his Baronial pile is a sixteenth-century tower house and elements from the thirteenth-century curtain-walled castle, including the gatehouse (centre left), still with its drawbridge slots.

Dean Castle

Kilmarnock, East Ayrshire
01563 554734 | www.eastayrshireleisure.com

TOWER-HOUSE CASTLE

A residence of the Boyds from the fourteenth to the eighteenth centuries. A rare, well-preserved example of a tower-house castle, where the tower house (left) still has its hall-block (right) standing proudly beside it. Probably built by Robert, the 1st Lord Boyd, who in 1466 became governor of Scotland during James III's minority. William, the 10th Lord, became Earl of Kilmarnock in 1661. Gutted by fire in 1735, it was lovingly restored by the 8th Lord Howard de Walden in the early twentieth century.

Delgatie Castle

Turriff, Aberdeenshire
01888 563479 | www.delgatiecastle.com

TOWER-HOUSE CASTLE

An impressive castle with an intriguing history. At its centre is the great tower house (left), built in the 1570s. The five-storey L-plan building is particularly noted for its exceptionally wide spiral stair rising through the building, its fine vaulted ceiling in the hall adorned with the Hay arms, and the painted ceilings in the upper chambers. The lower range (right) was added, and the tower substantially altered, c.1770, whilst later changes include the porch and bay window (far left), added in the 1840s. Delgatie's chief interest, however, lies in why it was built. At the Protestant Reformation (1560), many Aberdeenshire landowners, devout Catholics, were concerned for their safety. Some resorted to building strongly-defended tower houses. They included William Hay of Dronlaw and his wife, Lady Beatrice, daughter of the Earl of Errol. They invited the master mason, Alexander Crom, 1st of Auchry, to do precisely that. The Hays of Delgatie continued to tread a fine line between loyalty and treachery; one of them, Sir William, was executed alongside the Marquis of Montrose in 1650. After a period in the hands of others, Delgatie returned to the Hays after World War II, and became the Clan Hay Centre.

Dirleton Castle

Dirleton, near North Berwick, East Lothian
01620 850330 | www.historicenvironment.scot

ENCLOSURE CASTLE / TOWER-HOUSE CASTLE

For four centuries this great castle served as a residence for three noble families – the de Vauxes, the Haliburtons, and the Ruthvens. Built c.1240 for John de Vaux, steward of Alexander II's queen, Marie, his impressive curtain-walled castle closely resembles that built by Marie's father, Duke Enguerrand, at Coucy-le-Chateau, near Amiens, France. That, too, had boldly projecting drum towers, and John de Vaux built three at Dirleton, including the donjon, or keep, pictured here. In 1298, Edward I of England besieged it with stone-throwing artillery, causing great damage. After the Wars of Independence ended in 1356, the Haliburtons rebuilt it, including a new gatehouse (right) leading to their new lodging behind. The Ruthvens (later Earls of Gowrie) acquired it as a secondary residence c.1510, and following the 3rd Earl's execution in 1600, his widow and children lived here. They were the last noble residents. Soon after, the castle became a base for Royalists fighting Cromwell and they cut down the donjon by a whole storey to create a gun-battery. To no avail, for Cromwell's Roundheads captured it in 1651.

Dornoch Palace

Dornoch, Sutherland
01862 810216 | www.dornochcastlehotel.com

TOWER-HOUSE CASTLE

Close by the medieval cathedral, this four-storey tower
was part of the residence of the bishops of Caithness
from c.1500 to the Reformation in 1560. Thereafter it fell
into the hands of the Earls of Sutherland, and into hard
times. Caught up in the bloody feud between the
Gordon Earls of Sutherland and the Sinclair Earls of
Caithness, it was burnt in 1567 and left a ruin until the
Countess of Sutherland had it converted into the burgh's
courthouse and jail in 1810–14.

Doune Castle

Doune, near Stirling
01786 841742 | www.historicenvironment.scot

TOWER-HOUSE CASTLE

A powerfully impressive courtyard castle mostly of the later fourteenth century but incorporating earlier work. Built by Robert Stewart, Duke of Albany and brother of the ineffectual Robert III, the Duke of Albany effectively ruled Scotland until his death in 1420. The great gatehouse tower (left) housed his private lodging with a great hall (right), one of the most impressive medieval feasting halls in Scotland. After Albany's son's execution for treason in 1425, their stronghold reverted to the Crown.

Drum Castle

near Drumoak, Aberdeenshire
01330 700334 | www.nts.org.uk

TOWER-HOUSE CASTLE 👹 ✳️ ◼️

One of the oldest stone castles in NE Scotland, showing the transition from medieval keep to Jacobean tower house to Scots Baronial mansion. Built by Sir William Irwyn (Irvine) on being granted the estate by Robert the Bruce in 1323, following his appointment as forester (manager) of the royal forest of Drum. A closed-up, inward-looking building, it rises through four storeys to a corbelled-out parapet with open 'rounds' at each corner. There are few openings; the large, round-arched window was inserted in the 1870s. The tower was entered at first-floor level, and inside were a hall and lord's chamber, one above the other, with dark cellars below and chambers above. Whatever other buildings stood around it were swept away in the 1610s when Alexander Irvine, the 9th laird, added an L-shaped, three-storey wing adjacent (left), within a neat courtyard reached through an arched entrance. The courtyard was further developed in 1875–82 by Alexander Forbes Irvine, the 20th laird, designed by David Bryce and built in attractive coursed granite.

Drumcoltran Tower

near Kirkgunzeon, Dumfries & Galloway
0131 668 8600 | www.historicenvironment.scot

TOWER-HOUSE CASTLE

House of a cadet branch of the Maxwells, built in the later sixteenth century. Still roofed and showing internally how a Jacobean tower house could still provide a reasonably comfortable lairdly residence well into the eighteenth century. There is a cosy study at the head of the spiral stair. The Latin inscription above the entrance doorway is full of wisdom: 'Keep hidden what is secret; speak little; be truthful; avoid wine; remember death; be merciful.'

Drumlanrig Castle

near Carronbridge, Dumfries & Galloway
01848 331555 | www.drumlanrigcastle.co.uk

CASTELLATED MANSION

The hugely impressive castellated seat of the Dukes and Duchesses of Buccleuch and Queensberry. Built 1675–97 for William Douglas, 3rd Earl of Queensberry; he only ever slept one night here, before deciding he didn't like the place after all and returning to Sanquhar Castle. Bonnie Prince Charlie slept in one of its 120 rooms in 1745, during his withdrawal from Derby. The fine Queensberry Mausoleum is in nearby Durisdeer Kirk.

Duart Castle

near Craignure, Isle of Mull
01680 812309 | www.duartcastle.com

ENCLOSURE CASTLE / TOWER-HOUSE CASTLE

Everyone's idea of a Highland castle. Its formidable
stone curtain was built by the MacDougalls of Lorn in
the thirteenth century, and its great tower a century later,
by the MacLeans of Duart and Morvern. The rest
followed in the sixteenth and seventeenth centuries.
Falling into decay after the Jacobite Risings of the
eighteenth century. Sir Fitzroy MacLean, soldier, writer,
and politician, restored it to its former glory in 1911–12.

Duffus Castle

near Elgin, Moray
01667 460232 | www.historicenvironment.scot

MOTTE CASTLE / TOWER-HOUSE CASTLE

Built c.1150 by Freskin as a large motte-and-bailey castle.
His timber tower stood on the huge earthen motte
(right). His son William 'of Moray' founded Clan Murray.
By the time Andrew Moray co-led the Scots to victory
over the English at Stirling Bridge in 1297, Duffus was
owned by the Cheynes, Lords of Inverugie. They built the
square stone keep. However, when it started slipping
down the slope, they had to build a new residence down
in the bailey.

Dumbarton Castle

Dumbarton, near Glasgow
01389 732167 | www.historicenvironment.scot

OTHER

Dun Breattann means 'Fort of the Britons', and the twin peaks of Dumbarton Rock have a history reaching back to the Dark Ages 1500 years ago. It was known then as Alt Clut 'Rock of the Clyde', and from it ruled the kings of Strathclyde. In 870, a great Viking siege, led by Olaf and Ivar, resulted in its capture; 200 longships took the captives and booty back to Dublin. When Alexander II of Scotland built the royal castle c.1220, the border with Norway lay just 10 miles down the Clyde, and the castle's role then was as frontier stronghold. But the Battle of Largs, fought between Scotland and Norway in 1263, effectively ended Norway's sovereignty. Thereafter, the problem was the English, and the royal castle found a new role, serving as a postern, or back gate, into the kingdom. David II and Queen Joan (1333–4), and Mary Queen of Scots (1548) sheltered here prior to boarding vessels taking them to France and safety. During the troubled times of the seventeenth and eighteenth centuries, the Rock found a new role as garrison fortress. New accommodation was built and 'state-of-the-art' artillery defences erected. These included the Governor's House and King George's Battery, pictured here.

Dundonald Castle

Dundonald, near Troon, South Ayrshire
01563 851489 | www.historicenvironment.scot

TOWER-HOUSE CASTLE

The 'fort of Donald' has a history of fortification going back to prehistoric time. The eponymous Donald may probably be a king of Dark-Age Strathclyde. The impressive tower crowning the hill was built for Robert Stewart to mark his accession as Robert II in 1371. It had cavernous cellars with two superimposed feasting halls above, but oddly nowhere to sleep, unless we are missing a top floor. 'King Bob' died here in 1390, before the chamber tower (left) was added.

Dunfermline Palace

Dunfermline, Fife
01383 739026 | www.historicenvironment.scot

PALACE

There was a royal residence in the abbey from the outset in the twelfth century. David II (1323) and James I (1394) were both born here. In the 1580s, the abbey's former guest range was rebuilt as a fine palace for Anna of Denmark, James VI's queen. Her architect, William Schaw, made the most of the wonderful views over Pittencrieff Glen to the south, providing large, fine windows. In 1600 the queen gave birth here to the future Charles I.

Dunnottar Castle

near Stonehaven, Aberdeenshire
01569 762173 | www.dunnottarcastle.co.uk

TOWER-HOUSE CASTLE

There can be few castles as spectacularly sited as the ancestral seat of the Keiths, Earls Marischal of Scotland – on a lonely promontory thrusting into the chilly North Sea, and approachable only over a precipitous tongue of land. The castle is extensive. Passing through the heavily-defended entrance, up steps, past gunholed defences and through a darkened passage, one first reaches the castle's most impressive structure – a lofty, L-plan, early fifteenth-century tower house of four storeys (right). Here, for eight months in 1651–2, Scotland's ancient Crown Jewels were hidden from Cromwell's Roundheads, before being smuggled out under their noses to nearby Kinneff Kirk. Beyond the tower, an array of buildings of the sixteenth and seventeenth centuries (left), including a palace, chapel, and stables. Here, during the dreadful 'Killing Time' of the 1680s, many Covenanters (religious dissidents) were incarcerated. Some died here, whilst others escaped. Before the castle was built, the promontory was a Dark-Age stronghold, steeped in history and legend. History tells us that Donald II was killed here by Vikings in 900, whilst the Romance of Fergus recounts that it was home to a hideous old hag who guarded a magic shield.

Dunrobin Castle

near Golspie, Sutherland
01408 633177 | www.dunrobincastle.co.uk

TOWER-HOUSE CASTLE

A 'fairytale' castle overlooking the Sutherland coast. Robert, 6th Earl of Sutherland, is said to have built the oldest part, a tower house embedded deep within its walls, in the early 15th century – whence the name Dunrobin 'Robin (Robert)'s fort'. However, its origins may reach back to the twelfth century when Sutherland fell under the king of Norway's sway. The Sutherlands, descended from Freskin of Duffus, acquired the lands and the Earldom in the early thirteenth century. As with most Scottish tower-house castles, Dunrobin's tower was added to down the years, by other buildings, courtyards, and gardens, including in the seventeenth century by an L-plan range of three storeys. In the 1840s these were all dramatically subsumed when the new Duke of Sutherland, the former Earl of Stafford, asked the noted English architect, Sir Charles Barry – famous for designing the Houses of Parliament – to transform his residence into its present 'fairytale' appearance. Gutted by fire in 1915, when it was in use as a naval hospital, the castle was restored by another great architect, Sir Robert Lorimer, best known for his National Shrine in Edinburgh Castle.

Duns Castle

Duns, Berwickshire
01361 883211 | www.dunscastle.co.uk

CASTELLATED MANSION

The residence of the Hays of Drumelzier, who inherited the estate in 1696. Although the remnant of a fourteenth-century tower house lies within, the Scots Baronial pile we see today dates only from c.1820 when the family invited the famous architect, James Gillespie Graham, to remodel and extend it. The earthworks of a star-shaped artillery fort built in 1639 by General David Leslie's Covenanting Army lies on nearby Duns Law.

Dunstaffnage Castle

near Oban

01631 562465 | www.historicenvironment.scot

ENCLOSURE CASTLE / TOWER-HOUSE CASTLE

Built c.1220 by the MacDougalls to guard the approach into Argyll from the Firth of Lorn. A brute mass of masonry, with few openings. The corner towers were added c.1260, when Scotland and Norway, who ruled over the Hebrides, were at war. The MacDougalls lost their castle to Robert the Bruce in 1308, who installed the Campbells as keepers. The house rising above the battlements, added in 1725, was where, in 1746, Flora MacDonald was briefly held prisoner, after smuggling Bonnie Prince Charlie to safety.

Dunvegan Castle

Dunvegan, Isle of Skye
01470 521206 | www.dunvegancastle.com

TOWER-HOUSE CASTLE

Dunvegan is one of the oldest continuously inhabited castles in Scotland. Situated at the head of Loch Dunvegan, in northern Skye, from its battlements the eye can see across the wide waters of the Minch to the mountains on Harris, in the Western Isles. This was the domain of the chiefs of Clan MacLeod, and the sea-loch would once have been crowded with their birlinns (galleys). Clan MacLeod trace their roots back to Leod, son of Olaf 'the Black', Norse king of Man, in the twelfth century. Dunvegan has been their seat since the 1270s. The stronghold originally comprised a great tower, to which in the early sixteenth century Alasdair Crotach, 'hunchbacked Alasdair', added another, even taller, one, intriguingly known as the 'Fairy Tower' (left). Alasdair also built St Clement's Church, at Rodel, on Harris, where his splendid carved tomb can be seen. Much of what we see at Dunvegan dates to a major restoration between 1790 and 1850 by Norman 'the General' MacLeod and his son John Norman and grandson Norman, respectively the 23rd, 24th, and 25th Chiefs. Today, Hugh Magnus, the 30th Chief, resides therein.

Edinburgh Castle

Edinburgh
0131 225 9846 | www.edinburghcastle.gov.uk

ENCLOSURE CASTLE / PALACE

One of the most famous castles in the world. Sited on an extinct volcano, with a history reaching back to the Bronze Age. The oldest building is tiny St Margaret's Chapel, built in the 1130s by David I in memory of his mother. His castle suffered hugely in the Wars of Independence (1296-1356) and David II had almost entirely to rebuild it. The stump of his mighty David's Tower survives beneath the later Half-Moon Battery (centre). James IV built the majestic Great Hall in 1510, James V the Forewall Battery in the 1540s, and Regent Morton the Portcullis Gate and Half-Moon Battery for James VI, following the Lang Siege of 1571–3. Mary Queen of Scots gave birth to James VI & I in the palace (left) in 1566. All else is later, but still of considerable interest, most memorably the National War Memorial, in Crown Square, created from an eighteenth-century barracks in the 1920s. The castle also holds many treasures, including the ancient Scottish Crown Jewels, Mons Meg, the oldest cannon in the U.K., and three military museums. The world-famous Military Tattoo is held on the Esplanade each August.

Edzell Castle

Edzell, near Brechin, Angus
01356 648631 | www.historicenvironment.scot

TOWER-HOUSE CASTLE

A fine tower-house castle built by the 'lichtsome (carefree) Lindsays', Earls of Crawford, in the sixteenth century. A four-storey, L-plan tower (left) at one end of a two-storey range housing the entrance gateway and a feasting hall. Mary Queen of Scots and her Privy Council met here in 1562. In 1604, Sir David Lindsay added the remarkable walled garden, summerhouse, and bathhouse (now ruined). Sadly, the Lindsays had to sell their dream home in 1715 to pay off huge debts.

Eilean Donan Castle

Dornie, near Kyle of Lochalsh, Highlands
01599 555202 | www.eileandonancastle.com

TOWER-HOUSE CASTLE

One of Scotland's most photographed castles, originating in the thirteenth century as the stronghold of the Mackenzies of Kintail (later Earls of Seaforth). Despite its name – 'island of St Donan' – the place has a most unsaintly history. In 1331, the battlements were 'adorned' with the heads of 15 soldiers. Its end was equally bloody. In 1719, during a Jacobite Rising, gunpowder from a Royal Navy warship was used to blow the place to smithereens. The ruins were completely rebuilt by Col. John MacRae-Gilstrap in the early 1900s.

Elcho Castle

near Perth
01738 639998 | www.historicenvironment.scot

TOWER-HOUSE CASTLE

A charming tower house built in the later sixteenth century by the Wemyss family. Not their main residence – that lay at Wemyss, on the Fife coast – but a place in the country where they might relax and indulge in outdoor sports. The large, Z-plan tower demonstrates well the transition from castle to mansion made in Jacobean Scotland, combining an impressive exterior with a comfortable interior. The ground-floor entrance led to the kitchen and cellars, including a wine cellar, on the ground floor, and via a broad spiral stair to the spacious, well-lit hall and withdrawing chamber on the first floor. Two further stairs led to the upper floors, housing private chambers for the family, their household, and guests. Some of the original painted wall decoration survives. The gunholes at ground level and the cage grilles over the upper windows on the outside, and the yett (cross-barred gate) behind the front door weren't intended so much for defence, but to ward off undesirables, like thieves; this was an age before banks were invented. Elcho is an excellent example of the shift in Scottish architecture in Jacobean times, from the defensive to the domestic.

Falkland Palace

Falkland, near Glenrothes, Fife
01337 857397 | www.nts.org.uk

PALACE ♚ ❀ ▪

Attractively set in the heart of the historic burgh of
Falkland, and surrounded by the wonderful scenery of
the Lomond Hills. Falkland became a residence of the
royal family following Robert Stewart's accession as
Robert II in 1371. Ideally located within a rich hunting
park, it became a favoured place where the royal family
could escape the filth and intrigue of Edinburgh and
Stirling, and enjoy outdoor leisure pursuits. Both James
IV (1488–1513) and James V (1513–42) had a hand in
creating what we see today, most memorably the
eye-catching twin-towered gatehouse range (pictured),
emblazoned with the royal arms. The sumptuous Chapel
Royal on an upper floor still serves for worship, whilst
the Real (royal) tennis court, dating from 1539 and the
world's oldest court, is still used. James V died in the
palace in 1542, reputedly in the 'King's Room'. His only
child, Mary Queen of Scots, loved Falkland as did her
only child, James VI & I; he spent much of his
'hamecoming' to Scotland in 1617 here, thoroughly
enjoying the thrill of the chase.

Finlaggan Castle

near Ballygrant, Islay
www.islayinfo.com

OTHER

No ordinary castle this, for the two islands in Finlaggan
Loch – Eilean Mor ('big isle') and Eilean na Comhairle
('council isle') – were where the powerful MacDonalds,
Lords of the Isles, held their annual parliament. Descended
from Donald, grandson of the great Somerled, 'king of
the Isles', killed near Glasgow in 1164 fighting Malcolm
IV, the MacDonalds ruled supreme over the Hebrides
until finally overthrown by James IV in 1493.

Floors Castle

Kelso, Scottish Borders
01573 223333 | www.roxburghe.net

CASTELLATED MANSION

Scotland's largest inhabited castle, home of the Dukes
and Duchesses of Roxburghe. Although there is reputedly
an old tower on the site, the present vast mansion was
designed by William Adam and built in the 1720s for
John Kerr, the 1st Duke. William Playfair added the many
spires, turrets, and domes a century later. Somewhere in
the surrounding parkland in 1460 James II was killed,
whilst besieging mighty Roxburgh Castle, when one of
his cherished bombards exploded.

Fyvie Castle

Fyvie, near Turriff, Aberdeenshire
01651 891266 | www.nts.org.uk

TOWER-HOUSE CASTLE

One of the largest and finest examples of Scottish Renaissance architecture. Its five prominent towers enshrine five centuries of history, each named after one of the families who owned the castle – the Prestons, who acquired it in 1402, the Meldrums in 1433, the Setons in 1596, the Gordons in 1733, and finally the Leiths in 1889. The oldest, the Preston Tower (far right), dates from the early fifteenth century. The splendid array of wallhead details, including those finely sculpted corbel-tables, slender pepperpot turrets, crowstepped gables, and pedimented dormer windows, were part of a major remodelling c.1600 by Alexander Seton, Mary Queen of Scots's godson and James VI's Chancellor. The glorious Seaton Tower here on the south front (on the right of the picture), whose twin towers incorporate the entrance, has been described as 'the crowning triumph of Scottish Baronial architecture'. Internally, there is much to admire too, including the principal newel stair adorned with 22 coats of arms, the panelled charter room, and much fine plasterwork. The castle sits within a fine designed landscape with its own loch, laid out in the early eighteenth century.

Glamis Castle

Glamis, near Forfar, Angus
01307 840393 | www.glamis-castle.co.uk

TOWER-HOUSE CASTLE

A magnificent castellated confection, famed not just for its stunning architecture but also for its romantic association with Shakespeare's Macbeth; Malcolm II is said to have been slain by Macbeth at Glamis in 1034. Nothing in the present castle dates back quite that far. At its core is a great, later fourteenth-century rectangular tower house built by one of the Lyon family; they had newly married into the Royal House of Stewart. Sir Patrick Lyon was created 1st Lord Glamis in 1445. The 9th Lord became Earl of Kinghorne in 1606, and the 3rd Earl also became Earl of Strathmore in 1677. Down the generations the tower house grew, upwards and outwards. It was made L-shaped in the sixteenth century, and the round entrance tower and lower wings were added from the seventeenth century on. An exhausting 143 stairs take the visitor up from the basement vaults to the battlements high above. Glamis was the childhood home of Lady Elizabeth Bowes Lyon, the late Queen Elizabeth the Queen Mother, and Princess Margaret, her second child, was born here in 1930. The Bowes Lyons, Earls of Strathmore and Kinghorn, remain in residence today.

Glenbuchat Castle

near Kildrummy, Aberdeenshire
01667 460232 | www.historicenvironment.scot

TOWER-HOUSE CASTLE

Another residence of the ubiquitous Gordons, this in Strathdon. An interesting Z-plan tower house, built in 1590 by John Gordon of Cairnburrow to celebrate his marriage to Helen Carnegie, according to the inscription above the entrance door. The interior followed the standard Jacobean layout – a kitchen and cellars at ground level, an impressive hall on the first floor with a withdrawing chamber in an adjacent tower, and private rooms above. However, this was soon re-ordered. In 1701, the tower was purchased by John Gordon of Knockespock, who passed it to his son, also John. The latter divided the hall into two smaller rooms – a dining room and drawing room – and inserted a floor above to create further accommodation. The young John Gordon of Knockespock went on to become a great Jacobite soldier, who, as Brigadier-general John Gordon, led the Gordons and Farquharsons at Culloden in 1746. So scared of him was George II that it was said the monarch awoke in the night screaming in his broken German: 'De dread Glenbogged is goming!' 'Old Genbucket' died an exile in France.

Greenknowe Tower

Gordon, near Greenlaw, Scottish Borders
0131 668 8600 | www.historicenvironment.scot

TOWER-HOUSE CASTLE

A pleasing L-plan tower house, built for James Seton of
Touch and his second wife, Jane Edmonston, in 1581.
In the seventeenth century, the Pringles of Stichill
became owners. The green knoll on which it sits could
well be the site of the original castle of the Gordons,
'Cocks o the North'. They came first to the Borders prior
to relocating north in the fourteenth century. The village
of Gordon lies a stone's throw away to the east, and the
hamlet of Huntly a little to the west.

Haddo House

near Tarves, Aberdeenshire
01651 851440 | www.nts.org.uk

CASTELLATED MANSION

Nothing remains of the medieval castle of the Gordons of Haddo, destroyed during the Marquis of Montrose's Royalist campaigns of the 1640s. The present Palladian mansion was designed for William Gordon, 2nd Earl of Aberdeen, by the great William Adam in 1728. Somewhat plain by Adam's standards, the three-storey building was remodelled in the 1880s.

Hailes Castle

near East Linton, East Lothian
0131 668 8600 | www.historicenvironment.scot

HALL CASTLE / TOWER-HOUSE CASTLE

One of Scotland's oldest stone castles, built c.1240. A noble residence for over 300 years, serving first the Gourlays then the Hepburns. The Gourlays, from County Durham, served in the retinue of the powerful Balliols of Barnard Castle, and their castle shares similarities with those south of the Border. The lightly-fortified manor house comprised a central, two-storey hall block, with a taller tower at either end, one housing the kitchen and well, and the other (pictured left) the family's private chambers. All was built of squared blocks of red sandstone, with narrow round-headed windows. King John Balliol's downfall in 1296 led to the bitter Wars of Independence, and the Gourlays were disinherited. Their place at Hailes was taken by the Hepburns, retainers of the Earls of Dunbar. They rebuilt the damaged castle, adding a new curtain wall and lofty tower house (right). Their most famous son was James, 4th Earl of Bothwell, who became Mary Queen of Scots's third husband in 1566. Following his flight into exile the following year, Hailes fell into decay.

Hermitage Castle

near Newcastleton, Hawick, Scottish Borders
01387 376222 | www.historicenvironment.scot

HALL CASTLE / TOWER-HOUSE CASTLE

A vast, eerie ruin in Liddesdale, once known as the 'bloodiest valley in Britain'; hard by the English border where national strife and local feuding went hand in hand. The earthworks around it mostly belong to a mid thirteenth-century castle built by Lord Soules. The stone castle emerged a century later when Lord Dacre, a Cumbrian lord, built a fortified manor at the site. When the Black Douglases ousted him in 1371, they transformed his modest house into a huge, forbidding rectangular tower, with smaller towers projecting from each corner. The ground-floor entrance was blocked up and replaced by a strong first-floor doorway, whilst the battlements were given an unusual oversailing timber gallery reached through those small doorways near the top. Mary Queen of Scots almost lost her life here in 1566, whilst riding across the bleak moorland from Jedburgh to visit her lover, the Earl of Bothwell, himself recovering from being shot by a Border reiver (raider). In 1594 it was purchased by the Scotts of Branxholm; their descendants, the 4th and 5th Dukes of Buccleuch, repaired it in the early 1800s.

Hollows Tower

near Canonbie, Dumfries & Galloway
www.armstrong-clan.co.uk

TOWER-HOUSE CASTLE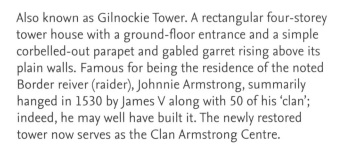

Also known as Gilnockie Tower. A rectangular four-storey tower house with a ground-floor entrance and a simple corbelled-out parapet and gabled garret rising above its plain walls. Famous for being the residence of the noted Border reiver (raider), Johnnie Armstrong, summarily hanged in 1530 by James V along with 50 of his 'clan'; indeed, he may well have built it. The newly restored tower now serves as the Clan Armstrong Centre.

Holyroodhouse, Palace of

Edinburgh
0131 556 5100 | www.royalcollection.org.uk

PALACE ✳ ■

The royal family had a lodging here from the abbey's foundation c.1128. As monasticism waned in the later fifteenth century, James IV began to encroach on their cloister. By the 1530s, James V had built an impressive palace (foreground) with eye-catching, projecting round towers. Here in 1566 Mary Queen of Scots's confidante, David Rizzio, was brutally murdered. A century later, Charles II added the present palace (beyond) after he returned from exile in 1660.

House of the Binns

near Bo'ness and Linlithgow
01506 834255 | www.nts.org.uk

COURTYARD CASTLE

Situated on hills offering fine views over the River Forth and the Pentland Hills. The medieval castle of the Livingstones of Kilsyth was purchased by the wealthy Edinburgh burgess, Thomas Dalyell, in 1612. He demolished the castle and built a large castellated mansion in its stead. Three storeys high to its crenellated parapet, with impressively large windows and fine interiors, including rooms decorated with ornate plaster ceilings intended to grace a visit by Charles I that never materialized. His son, the larger-than-life 'General Tam o the Binns', fought for Charles II at the Battle of Worcester in 1651, where he was taken prisoner. Escaping from the Tower of London, he fled abroad and served with the Russian Tsar, earning a formidable, if ruthless, reputation. On Charles's return to his throne, General Tam too returned to Scotland, becoming commander of the king's army here. He defeated the Covenanters at Rullion Green in 1666, and in 1681 mustered a new cavalry regiment here at The Binns – the Royal Regiment of Scots Dragoons (later the Royal Scots Greys). His descendant, Tam Dalyell (d.2017) was equally redoubtable, but he did his fighting on the floor of the House of Commons.

Houston House

Uphall, near Livingston, West Lothian
0344 879 9043 | www.macdonaldhotels.co.uk

TOWER-HOUSE CASTLE

Prettily surrounded by woodland, Houston perfectly shows how a much altered and much extended late-medieval tower house can still serve as agreeably pleasing accommodation today. Sir John Shairp (Sharp), James VI's advocate, built the first element, a tall, unturreted L-plan tower house, c.1600, his family having acquired the property from the Houstons c.1570. Later in the century they extended it with ranges enclosing a rectangular courtyard. Subsequent additions included a small stair tower in the early eighteenth century and an entrance porch a century later. The Sharps finally sold in 1945, and the castle has served as a wonderfully relaxing hotel ever since. The new owners added their own, sympathetically designed, extensions in the 1960s.
Of the older medieval castle, built for the Houstons prior to the Sharps' arrival, there is now no trace, and very little trace of the motte-and-bailey castle built by Freskin, the Fleming, in the twelfth century, prior to his relocating to Duffus Castle, in far-off Moray.

Huntingtower Castle

near Perth

01738 627231 | www.historicenvironment.scot

TOWER-HOUSE CASTLE

A residence of the Ruthvens, Earls of Gowrie, and then of the Murrays, Earls of Tullibardine. When built in the fifteenth century it comprised two towers almost touching. Mary Queen of Scots honeymooned here in 1565 with Lord Darnley. The towers were formed into one by the Murrays in the later seventeenth century, to make their residence more like a country mansion. Inside is some of the oldest painted decoration in Scotland, dating from the first half of the sixteenth century.

Huntly Castle

Huntly, Aberdeenshire
01466 793191 | www.historicenvironment.scot

ENCLOSURE CASTLE / TOWER-HOUSE CASTLE

A noble ruin, noted both for its architecture and its
eventful history. Built where the rivers Bogie and Don
meet, it shows the development of the castle in Scotland,
from the twelfth-century motte-and-bailey, through the
tower house of the later Middle Ages, to the stately
palace of Jacobean times. The palace (pictured) impresses
most today. Remodelled by the 4th Earl, c.1550, it was
wonderfully embellished by the 1st Marquis, c.1600,
with an unparalleled array of oriel windows.

Inveraray Castle

near Inveraray, Argyll
01499 302203 | www.inveraray-castle.com

CASTELLATED MANSION

A huge, four-square castellated mansion, with large round towers at the corners, built for Archibald Campbell, 3rd Duke of Argyll, in the 1740s. He laid out the pretty planned town of Inveraray at the same time. The Campbell chiefs relocated here from Innis Chonnell, their island lair on Loch Awe, in the mid fifteenth century. Nothing remains of this first castle, for the 3rd Duke demolished it immediately on completing his new residence.

Jedburgh, Queen Mary's House

Jedburgh, Scottish Borders
01835 863331 | www.jedburgh.org.uk

TOWER-HOUSE CASTLE

Tower houses stood in towns as well as out in the countryside. This early sixteenth-century T-plan tower was one of six that stood in Jedburgh. Built for the Scotts of Ancrum, it is famous for being where, in October 1566, Mary Queen of Scots lay seriously ill, having fallen off her horse on returning over the bleak moorland from lonely Hermitage Castle where her lover, the Earl of Bothwell, lay recovering from being shot. The tower is now the Mary Queen of Scots Visitor Centre.

Kelburn Castle

near Fairlie, north Ayrshire
01475 568685 | www.kelburnestate.com

TOWER-HOUSE CASTLE

Not many Scottish castles can claim to have been in the same family throughout their existence – Kelburn can. The Boyles emerge on record c.1200, and one of them helped fend off the Norsemen at the Battle of Largs, fought nearby in 1263. Part of their first castle is said to lie at the core of the lofty, sixteenth-century, Z-plan tower house (right) that today dominates the site. Although much changed within, externally the tower retains its Jacobean appearance, including slender corner turrets, steep crowstepped gables, and a high stair tower terminating in a conical-roofed belvedere out of whose window Rapunzel could have let down her hair. David Boyle of Kelburn, Scotland's treasurer-depute, became Earl of Glasgow in 1703, and to celebrate he built a large mansion (left) beside his ancestral seat. In the 1880s, his descendant, the 7th Earl, extended it even further before becoming Governor of New Zealand. But what about that graffiti adorning the old tower today? It was a temporary measure taken by Lord Glasgow in 2007 to disguise the failing cement render covering the walls. The work of four Brazilian artists, it is still there.

Kellie Castle

near Pittenweem, Fife
01333 720271 | www.nts.org.uk

TOWER-HOUSE CASTLE

Set amid the lush countryside of the East Neuk of Fife,
Kellie is one of Scotland's finest late-medieval castles.
It was mostly built by the Oliphants, who held the estate
from the 1350s until 1613. Over the course of the
sixteenth century, they progressively built a fine, spacious
castellated residence. At its core a three-storey central
block (right) complemented by three large towers rising to
five floors and topped with pretty conical-roofed turrets.
In 1613, the Oliphants had to sell Kellie. The lucky buyer
was Sir Thomas Erskine of Gogar, whom James VI made
Earl of Kellie in 1619. Sir Thomas had helped his king
escape the clutches of the 3rd Earl of Gowrie in the
infamous 'Gowrie Conspiracy' of 1600. He also played a
leading role in King James's 'hamecoming' to Scotland
in 1617, to celebrate his Golden Jubilee. In anticipation
of His Majesty's visit, Sir Thomas upgraded his new
home, including installing some of the earliest ornate
plaster ceilings seen in Scotland; they are still there.
Abandoned in 1829, Kellie was leased in 1878 to a
Professor Lorimer and restored. His son, the noted
architect Robert Lorimer, grew up here.

Kilchurn Castle

north end of Loch Awe, near Dalmally, Argyll & Bute
0131 668 8600 | www.historicenvironment.scot

TOWER-HOUSE CASTLE

On Loch Awe, with Ben Cruachan as backdrop, this was
'Campbell's Kingdom'. Colin Campbell, Ist Lord of
Glenorchy, built the lofty tower house at one corner of
an irregular-shaped curtain wall c.1450. Colin, 6th Lord,
added the corner towers before relocating to Balloch
(now Taymouth), in Perthshire. In the troubled later
seventeenth century, John Campbell, 1st Earl of
Breadalbane, added a barracks for his 200-strong private
army – now the oldest surviving barracks in Britain.

Kildrummy Castle

Kildrummy, Aberdeenshire
01975 571331 | www.historicenvironment.scot

ENCLOSURE CASTLE

Built in the thirteenth century by the mighty Earls of Mar. A great curtain-walled castle with large towers projecting from it; the 'Warden's Tower' (left) is now the only one standing almost to full height. Beside it is the castle chapel (centre) lit by three lancets. Edward I of England stayed here in 1296 and 1303, and may have had the gatehouse built, for it is almost identical to that at Harlech. In 1715, the 6th Earl of Mar began the third Jacobite Rising here.

Kilravock Castle

Croy, near Nairn
www.kilravock.com

TOWER-HOUSE CASTLE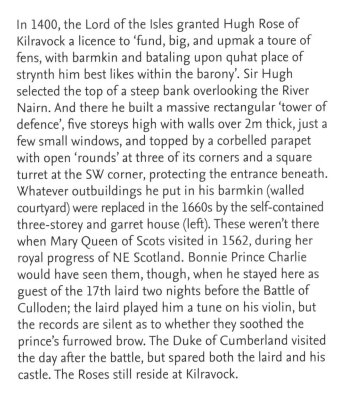

In 1400, the Lord of the Isles granted Hugh Rose of Kilravock a licence to 'fund, big, and upmak a toure of fens, with barmkin and bataling upon quhat place of strynth him best likes within the barony'. Sir Hugh selected the top of a steep bank overlooking the River Nairn. And there he built a massive rectangular 'tower of defence', five storeys high with walls over 2m thick, just a few small windows, and topped by a corbelled parapet with open 'rounds' at three of its corners and a square turret at the SW corner, protecting the entrance beneath. Whatever outbuildings he put in his barmkin (walled courtyard) were replaced in the 1660s by the self-contained three-storey and garret house (left). These weren't there when Mary Queen of Scots visited in 1562, during her royal progress of NE Scotland. Bonnie Prince Charlie would have seen them, though, when he stayed here as guest of the 17th laird two nights before the Battle of Culloden; the laird played him a tune on his violin, but the records are silent as to whether they soothed the prince's furrowed brow. The Duke of Cumberland visited the day after the battle, but spared both the laird and his castle. The Roses still reside at Kilravock.

Kinnaird Castle

near Brechin, Angus
01674 810240 | www.southesk.co.uk

CASTELLATED MANSION

Hidden somewhere within this splendid nineteenth-century castellated mansion could well be fabric from a real medieval castle. Way back in the thirteenth century, the Kinnaird estate was held by the Carnegies. Duthac Carnegie was killed fighting the MacDonald Lords of the Isles at Harlaw, Aberdeenshire, in 1411, Walter Carnegie fought against the Earl of Crawford at Brechin in 1452, whilst John Carnegie fell alongside his king, James IV, at Flodden in 1513, fighting the English. One of these built a tower house that may conceivably survive in the present east tower (right). James VI, Charles I, and Charles II all enjoyed stays here, hunting in the 1300 acres of walled parkland. The present impressive 'castle' dates from the 1790s when the architect, James Playfair, built a large mansion for Sir David Carnegie. Sixty years later, it was remodelled by the architect David Bryce in the French Baronial style, with a south front (pictured) dominated by a central turreted tower and with square towers at either end. Today, Kinnaird is a seat of the Duke and Duchess of Fife, descended from those medieval Carnegies.

Kinnaird Head Castle

Fraserburgh, Aberdeenshire
0131 668 8600 | www.historicenvironment.scot

TOWER-HOUSE CASTLE

Built in the mid sixteenth century by the Frasers of Philorth,
part of their grand scheme to make the fishing village of
Faithlie into a thriving port, which they named Fraserburgh.
A rectangular tower with open 'rounds' at the corners of
its corbelled-out wallhead. In 1786 the newly-created
Northern Lighthouse Board built a lighthouse inside,
designed by Thomas Smith. Scotland's first lighthouse,
its 17 reflectors gave it a range of over 12 miles.

Kirkwall, Bishop's Palace

Kirkwall, Orkney
01856 871918 | www.historicenvironment.scot

HALL CASTLE

A remarkable survival from the twelfth century – a
hall-house castle built beside St Magnus' Cathedral.
Both were created by Bishop William 'the Old', crusading
friend of Earl Rognvald. The first-floor hall and chamber
can still be made out where, in 1263, Hakon IV of Norway
breathed his last, after having led a huge armada into
the Firth of Clyde to try to overthrow Alexander III of
Scotland. Three years later, his son Magnus 'Barelegs'
ceded the entire Hebrides to Scotland.

Kirkwall, Earl's Palace

Kirkwall, Orkney
01856 871918 | www.historicenvironment.scot

TOWER-HOUSE CASTLE

A building of extraordinary refinement, spacious and masterly in its planning. The Earl's Palace was built by Patrick Stewart, Earl of Orkney and Lord of Shetland, c.1606. Known as 'Black Patie', the tyrannical Patrick ruled the Northern Isles with an iron fist from 1592 until his execution in Edinburgh 23 years later. It was declared at his trial that he used slave labour to build his palaces here and at Birsay, and his Shetland seat at Scalloway. It incorporated the twelfth-century Bishop's Palace within the large complex. The palace still has the power to impress, particularly the frontal facade with its array of oriel windows, corbelled turrets and elaborate entrance. The building internally expresses the owner's obsession with privacy and security, for his own apartment lay well away from those of his household officials and honoured guests. After Earl Patrick's demise, the palace was used by the Bishops of Orkney until episcopacy was finally abolished in the Church of Scotland in 1688.

Kisimul Castle

Castlebay, Isle of Barra, Outer Hebrides
01871 810313 | www.historicenvironment.scot

TOWER-HOUSE CASTLE

Caisteal Chaosmuil, meaning 'castle of the rock of the small bay', is testament to the nature of Gaelic lordship in the Middle Ages. The island fastness in Castle Bay was the stronghold of the Macneils of Barra, who claimed descent from the legendary Niall of the Nine Hostages, high king of Ireland in the fifth century. Tradition tells of the Macneils settling on Barra in the eleventh century, but it was only in 1427 that Gilleonan Macneil comes on record as the first lord. He probably built the curtain-walled castle, as well as the 'crew house' in its shadow for his personal galley and boatmen. The sea coursed through Macneil veins, and a descendant, Ruari 'the Turbulent', was arrested for piracy of an English ship in the late 1500s. Heavy debts forced the Macneil chiefs to sell Barra in 1838, but the 45th chief, Robert Lister Macneil, repurchased the estate in 1937 and set about restoring his ancestral seat.

Lauriston Castle

Edinburgh
0131 336 2060 | www.edinburghmuseums.org.uk

TOWER-HOUSE CASTLE

An impressive sixteenth-century tower house (left), built by the Napiers of Merchiston, to which a fine, two-storeyed extension was added in the 1820s, designed by William Burn. The residence has had a succession of owners since the Napiers, including the Cants, Dalgleishes, Laws (who built the extension), Allans, Rutherfords, Crawfords, and Reids. The Reids presented the house and extensive grounds to the City of Edinburgh, to be enjoyed by all.

Leith Hall

Kennethmont, near Huntly, Aberdeenshire
01464 831216 | www.nts.org.uk

TOWER-HOUSE CASTLE

A comfortable mansion in a fine landscape setting. At its
core, a later seventeenth-century tower house (left), three
storeys high, with projecting turrets at each corner.
Now forming a courtyard complex of eighteenth- and
nineteenth-century ranges, entered through a fine
pedimented gateway, flanked at the ends by pretty drum
towers. All this was the work of the Leith family, who
owned it throughout its history, until entrusting it to the
National Trust for Scotland in 1945.

Lennoxlove House

near Haddington, East Lothian
01620 823720 | www.lennoxlove.com

TOWER-HOUSE CASTLE

Lennoxlove was originally called Lethington. The Maitlands held it from 1345 to 1682. The oldest part is the L-plan tower house (foreground), built in the fourteenth century, probably by the first Maitland. As his descendants extended southward, so the original tower was altered to suit. New fenestration was introduced, including that tall window, and the interiors graced by new fireplaces, panelling, and plasterwork. Its most famous resident, William Maitland, Mary Queen of Scots's secretary, was involved in the plot to murder her second husband, Lord Darnley. At his death, Lethington passed to the Maitlands of Thirlestane; John Maitland, Duke of Lauderdale, Secretary of Scotland 1661–82, was born here in 1616. At his death, Lethington not only changed hands but also its name. In 1947, the 14th Duke of Hamilton bought it as a permanent replacement for Hamilton Palace, demolished in 1921. Lennoxlove is full of treasures, from the death-mask of Mary Queen of Scots, through a marvellous collection of portraits and porcelain, to memorabilia associated with Nigel Tranter, novelist and author of the fine five-volume The Fortified House in Scotland.

Lews Castle

Stornoway, Isle of Lewis
www.lews-castle.co.uk

CASTELLATED MANSION

Caisteal Leòdhais, overlooking Stornoway harbour, is another of those impressive Victorian 'castles' so beloved of Scotland's great landowners. In this instance the builder was Sir James Matheson, who made his millions from the lucrative opium trade with China; Jardine Matheson Holdings still operates today. On returning to his native Scotland in 1843, Matheson purchased the entire island of Lewis for over £500,000, and began a programme of improvements. These included inviting the Glasgow architect, Charles Wilson, to design his island home – a three-storey Tudor-esque 'fort', complete with corbelled-out crenellated battlements, topped by round and square turrets. Matheson also had the rough grazing around it cleared of tenants and landscaped into a woodland park. In 1918, another wealthy entrepreneur, William Lever, Lord Leverhume, the 'soap baron', purchased the island and castle. He extended it even further, and installed electricity, central heating, and the telephone. In 1923, shortly before his death, he bequeathed it to the people of Lewis. After serving as a college and school, it has just reopened as a museum, cultural centre, and hotel.

Linlithgow Palace

Linlithgow, West Lothian
01506 842896 | www.historicenvironment.scot

PALACE   ■

Majestic royal palace of the Stewarts. Begun by James I
in 1424, it became a pleasure palace for the Stewart
monarchs. The queens especially liked its tranquillity and
fresh air, and the palace served as a royal nursery for
James V (born 1512) and Mary Queen of Scots (born 1542).
Falling into decline after James VI moved the royal court
to London in 1603, its end came shortly before Culloden
when Redcoats billeted here accidently set the place ablaze.

Loch Doon Castle

near Dalmellington, Dumfries & Galloway
0131 668 8600 | www.historicenvironment.scot

ENCLOSURE CASTLE

Built in the late thirteenth century by an Earl of Carrick,
maybe Robert the Bruce himself before he became
King of Scots in 1306. A secondary castle to their chief
seat, Turnberry Castle, on the Ayrshire coast, the 11-sided
stone curtain-wall originally stood on an island in the
loch. In 1935 it was taken down and re-erected on the
nearby shore, prior to the creation of a hydro-electric
scheme that raised the water level.

Lochleven Castle

on an island in Loch Leven, near Kinross, Perth & Kinross
01577 862670 | www.historicenvironment.scot

TOWER-HOUSE CASTLE

One of Scotland's most famous castles, dominating an island in Loch Leven. The curtain wall around the tower house was possibly built by the English during the Wars of Independence (1296–1356); a tale tells of William Wallace capturing the island fastness and killing all 30 'Inglismen' he found there. After the Wars, the Douglases acquired the island and built the lofty tower. Rectangular in shape and five storeys high, its unusually high original entrance door, 5m above the ground, may have had more to do with the Douglases fearing flooding as much as the English. By the time Mary Queen of Scots came here, the tower had been re-ordered, probably to house her in suitable style. She first visited in 1561 as a guest of Sir William Douglas, but returned in 1567 as his prisoner. Her cell was on the fourth floor, above the hall, and visitors can still see the window that was converted into a tiny oratory for her. She was compelled to abdicate here in favour of her son, James VI. She also miscarried twins here; her doctor resided in the room above. It was there she disguised herself prior to escaping in May 1568.

Lochranza Castle

Lochranza, Isle of Arran
0131 668 8600 | www.historicenvironment.scot

HALL CASTLE / TOWER-HOUSE CASTLE

An unexpectedly fascinating castle. Outwardly, it looks a typical late-medieval tower house. On closer inspection, we find an early thirteenth-century hall house embedded within, built by one of the MacSweens, Lords of Knapdale, whose chief seat was Castle Sween. Lochranza probably gave them a secure base on the east side of the Kilbrannon Sound. The Montgomeries, Earls of Eglinton, rebuilt it in the sixteenth century.

MacLellan's Castle

Kirkcudbright, Dumfries & Galloway
01557 331856 | www.historicenvironment.scot

TOWER-HOUSE CASTLE

One of Scotland's finest sixteenth-century town houses, even in its roofless state. A large, L-plan tower – it had over 15 family rooms – completed in 1582 for Sir Thomas MacLellan of Bombie and his second wife Grisel Maxwell. Sir Thomas, provost of Kirkcudbright, was one of James VI's gentlemen of the bedchamber; the king visited him in 1587. One of its delights is the laird's lug behind the hall fireplace, where the laird eavesdropped on his guests!

Menstrie Castle

Menstrie, Clackmananshire, central Scotland
01259 211701 | www.nts.org.uk

TOWER-HOUSE CASTLE

Standing now somewhat incongruously in a housing estate. Built c.1560 by the Alexander family, owners since the later fifteenth century, it took the form of a modest, L-plan house two storeys and a garret high. During the seventeenth century, this was substantially extended when a new, long wing (left) was built out from the tower, and a walled courtyard formed behind, entered through the fine round-arched doorway. Its most famous resident was Sir William Alexander, a friend of James VI, born here in 1575. Becoming a privy councillor in 1615, then principal secretary in 1626, Charles I created him Earl of Stirling in 1633, during his coronation visit. For his own residence, Sir William created a splendid town house on the street leading to Stirling Castle, now known as Argyll's Lodging. Sadly, he died a bankrupt in London in 1644. Menstrie passed to the Holbornes in 1648, then the Abercrombies in 1719. But they stayed barely three decades before moving to Tullibody, leaving Menstrie empty. It was saved from destruction only after a public campaign in the 1950s inspired by the Scottish actor, Moultrie Kelsall.

Morton Castle

Morton Loch, near Carronbridge, Dumfries & Galloway
0131 668 8600 | www.historicenvironment.scot

HALL CASTLE

Hidden away in the Nithsdale hills is this gem of a castle.
Who built it and why is a mystery. Our best guess is
Sir Thomas Randolph, Lord of Morton and Robert the
Bruce's nephew; he led the audacious night assault on
English-held Edinburgh Castle in 1314, shortly before
the great Battle of Bannockburn. However, the
architectural detail points the finger of suspicion at an
Englishman, and it could have been built by a henchman
of Edward I 'Hammer of the Scots'. Nithsdale and
Annandale were effectively under English rule during the
Wars of Independence (1296–1356). Morton is termed a
'hall castle' because it comprised a large first-floor
feasting hall (centre left) with a chamber tower at one
end housing the lord's private lodging (right) and an
impressive twin-towered gatehouse at the other (seen
rising above the trees). The castle was probably among
those slighted following David II's return from captivity
in the Tower of London in 1356. Although the loch looks
as though it dates with the castle, it was actually created
in the nineteenth century to add enchantment to the
noble ruin.

Mount Stuart

near Rothesay, Isle of Bute
01700 503877 | www.mountstuart.com

CASTELLATED MANSION

A monumental Victorian extravaganza, encased externally in fanciful architecture and positively dripping with decoration within. One of the finest architectural creations of John Crichton-Stuart, 3rd Marquis of Bute, who with his vast wealth created not just Mount Stuart but also Cardiff Castle and Castel Coch in South Wales. Designed by Robert Rowand Anderson and built after a fire had destroyed its far more humble predecessor in 1877.

Muness Castle

near Uyeasound, Unst, Shetland
0131 668 8600 | www.historicenvironment.scot

TOWER-HOUSE CASTLE

The most northerly castle in the British Isles. A ruined
Z-plan castle built in 1598 for Laurence Bruce of
Cultmalindie, an incomer from Perthshire. Three storeys
high with a round tower at opposing corners. Fleeing
from involvement in a murder, Bruce fell out with the
tyrannical Earl Patrick, Lord of Shetland, but withstood a
siege in 1608; the gunholes under the windows may
have helped. In 1713 it was being used to store cargo
from a shipwrecked Dutch East Indiaman.

Neidpath Castle

Peebles, Scottish Borders
01875 870201 | www.neidpathcastle.co.uk

TOWER-HOUSE CASTLE

Impressively situated beside a twist in the River Tweed, a short distance upstream from the royal burgh of Peebles. One of the oldest tower houses in Scotland, built in the late fourteenth century by Sir William Hay of Locherworth, sheriff of Peebles, or his son Thomas. L-shaped on plan and rising through five storeys, its interior is noted for its heavy stone vaults over three of its floors. The grim pit-prison and well in the basement are legacies from its fourteenth-century origins. Substantially replanned in the sixteenth century, and further improved in the seventeenth century, to which date belong the fine wood panelling in the upper floors and most of the courtyard ranges. By the time James Grose, the antiquarian, visited in 1797 the building was abandoned as a residence and fast falling into ruin. The rot was stopped in 1810 when the Earls of Wemyss and March acquired it and converted it for estate workers' accommodation. In the later twentieth century, the 12th Earl developed it as a visitor attraction. Its bewitching interior is said to be haunted by Jean Douglas, 'the Maid of Neidpath', who apparently died of unrequited love here in the eighteenth century.

Newark Castle

Port Glasgow, near Greenock, central Scotland
01475 741858 | www.historicenvironment.scot

TOWER-HOUSE CASTLE

Gracing the southern shore of the Clyde estuary is the tower-house residence of a junior branch of the Maxwells. Built by George Maxwell of Finlaystone as a tower-house castle c.1480, only its tower and gatehouse survive. The castle was completely transformed a century later by Sir Patrick Maxwell into the remarkable Renaissance mansion we see today. Here on the outside are the slender pepperpot turrets, pedimented dormer windows, and crowstepped gables such as were then becoming 'all the rage', whilst the interior has some fascinating features, including a unique bedchamber complete with en-suite loo and walk-in sleeping cupboard. Sir Patrick's castle may have been a nice piece of work, but he himself wasn't, murdering several neighbours and even his own kin. His most sorry victim was his poor wife, Lady Margaret Crawford, who he brutally attacked and locked up in an upstairs chamber for six months. She eventually escaped but her husband was never brought to justice. The castle, for long imprisoned by shipyards, has recently re-emerged to take its place in the Port Glasgow scene once more.

Noltland Castle

near Pierowall, Westray, Orkney
01856 841815 | www.historicenvironment.scot

TOWER-HOUSE CASTLE

One of Scotland's most sinister-looking strongholds, chiefly because of the 70+ wide-mouthed gunholes piercing its walls. The inscription over the entrance chillingly reads: 'When I see the blood I will pass over you in the night'. Built by Gilbert Balfour, one of Mary Queen of Scots's household, in the 1560s. Implicated in the murders of Cardinal Beaton (1546) and Lord Darnley (1567), after his queen fled to England in 1568, he fled to Sweden, leaving his Orcadian bolthole unfinished.

Orchardton Tower

near Dalbeattie, Dumfries & Galloway
0131 668 8600 | www.historicenvironment.scot

TOWER-HOUSE CASTLE

Scotland's only circular tower house, built by the Cairns family c.1450. The reason for the unique shape is a mystery. In most other respects, it is typical. It had a first-floor entrance (the one pictured led only into a vaulted cellar), and beside it (right) stood a hall block. The tower was remodelled in the later sixteenth century, probably by its new Maxwell owners. They abandoned the place in the eighteenth century for a new residence nearby, Orchardton House.

Ravenscraig Castle

Kirkcaldy, Fife
0131 668 8600 | www.historicenvironment.scot

TOWER-HOUSE CASTLE

Begun in 1460 by James II as a gift for his queen Marie of Gueldres. Within months, James was dead, killed at the siege of Roxburgh, but his widow continued with the work. Whether she stayed there before her own death in 1463 is not known. If she had done, she would have resided in the lofty west tower that still dominates the complex; entered at first-floor level, it housed four floors of accommodation. Beside it was a first-floor hall above a heavily-guarded entrance. The lower east tower housed rooms for the household. In the seaward-facing courtyard behind were kitchens, bakehouse, and brewhouse. Because of its massively thick walls bristling with gunholes, the castle was long regarded more as a coastal artillery defence against the English than a house for royalty. Closer inspection reveals that none of the gunholes were original, but date from the time of the Sinclair Earls of Caithness, granted the castle in 1470 in return for resigning the Earldom of Orkney and Lordship of Shetland to the Crown. The fulmars nesting here are now 'kings of the castle'.

Rothesay Castle

Rothesay, Isle of Bute
01700 502691 | www.historicenvironment.scot

ENCLOSURE CASTLE

Owned by the Stewarts throughout its 800-year history, firstly the hereditary High Stewarts until 1371, and thereafter by the Royal Stewarts; Prince Charles is the current Duke of Rothesay. The castle was built c.1200 by Alan, the 2nd High Steward, as a defence against the Norsemen. From his time belong the water-filled moat and the high stone curtain wall, unique in Scotland in being circular in form. Despite these defences, the Norsemen twice successfully stormed it, in 1230 and 1263, though they quickly lost it again. After the latter, the 4th High Steward added four great drum towers projecting from the curtain, noted for their tall, slender arrow-slits. They weren't needed. In 1266, Magnus IV of Norway ceded the Hebrides back to Scotland, and these Viking descendants were never seen in the west again. When the 7th High Steward became Robert II in 1371, Rothesay became a royal castle. James IV and V remodelled it, building a chapel to St Michael within and the impressive rectangular gatehouse (left).

Roxburgh Castle

near Kelso, Scottish Borders
01573 223333

ENCLOSURE CASTLE / OTHER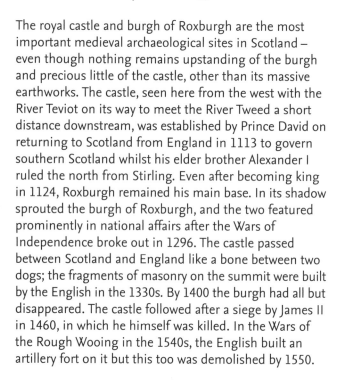

The royal castle and burgh of Roxburgh are the most important medieval archaeological sites in Scotland – even though nothing remains upstanding of the burgh and precious little of the castle, other than its massive earthworks. The castle, seen here from the west with the River Teviot on its way to meet the River Tweed a short distance downstream, was established by Prince David on returning to Scotland from England in 1113 to govern southern Scotland whilst his elder brother Alexander I ruled the north from Stirling. Even after becoming king in 1124, Roxburgh remained his main base. In its shadow sprouted the burgh of Roxburgh, and the two featured prominently in national affairs after the Wars of Independence broke out in 1296. The castle passed between Scotland and England like a bone between two dogs; the fragments of masonry on the summit were built by the English in the 1330s. By 1400 the burgh had all but disappeared. The castle followed after a siege by James II in 1460, in which he himself was killed. In the Wars of the Rough Wooing in the 1540s, the English built an artillery fort on it but this too was demolished by 1550.

Ruthven Castle

near Kingussie, Highlands
www.historicenvironment.scot

ENCLOSURE CASTLE / OTHER

A large natural mound, dominated by military buildings of the early eighteenth century. The site was first fortified in the thirteenth century by the powerful Comyns, Lords of Badenoch. In the later fourteenth century it was in the hands of the infamous Alexander Stewart, 'the Wolf of Badenoch', who in 1390 descended on Elgin Cathedral and set it alight. His resulting downfall saw the castle fall into ruin, but the Gordon Earls of Huntly rebuilt it in the later sixteenth century. Of these castles nothing remains except a well, discovered by excavation in 1983. Today the mound supports a barracks built for George I's government forces in the wake of the 1715 Jacobite Rising. One of four built in the Highlands, it comprised two piles of barracks facing each other across a central courtyard and defined by an enclosure wall loopholed for muskets. Two small projecting angle-towers housed officers' quarters. The single-storey building outside the wall (left) was a stable-block, added in 1734 at the instruction of General Wade, for the use of dragoons patrolling his new military road from Perth to Inverness.

St Andrews Castle

St Andrews, Fife
01334 477196 | www.historicenvironment.scot

ENCLOSURE CASTLE

Residence of the bishops of St Andrews from the twelfth century. Most of what remains dates from a rebuilding by Bishop Trail (d.1401). The castle illustrates the power and wealth of Scotland's leading clerics. The gruesome bottle dungeon was where Cardinal Beaton's murdered body was dumped in 1546 and where John Knox was imprisoned shortly after. The mine and counter-mine dug during the bitter siege of 1547 are the finest of their kind in Europe.

Scalloway Castle

Scalloway, Mainland, Shetland
01856 841815 | www.historicenvironment.scot

TOWER-HOUSE CASTLE

Built c.1600 for Patrick Stewart, Lord of Shetland, as his seat there. A large, Z-plan tower house, crowned at the corners by impressive corbelled-out turrets. Internally, it has an innovative scale-and-platt stair rising to the first floor rather than the traditional spiral stair. 'Black Patie' (Black Patrick) was deeply unpopular with Shetlanders, mainly because they were made to do forced labour, including building his castle. He finally got his 'come-uppence' in 1615 when he was executed on 'the Maiden' in Edinburgh.

Scone Palace

near Scone, Perth
01738 552300 | www.scone-palace.co.uk

CASTELLATED MANSION

Scone Palace itself is not old, but the site it occupies is steeped in history. The present house dates from 1803–12. David Murray, 3rd Earl of Mansfield, invited the architect, William Atkinson, to substantially recast an early seventeenth-century tower built by his forebear, David Murray of Gospatrie, cup-bearer to James VI, in the new, fashionable Georgian Gothic style. Atkinson's large but low-key castellated edifice is imposing externally and fascinating internally, not least its long gallery, almost 45m in length. But it is the site on which it stands that holds most fascination. Scone was the ancient king-making centre of the Picts and Scots. In 1803, the 3rd Earl tidied up the ancient Moot Hill where inauguration ceremonies took place on the famous Stone of Scone (Stone of Destiny); these included Macbeth (1140), Robert the Bruce (1306), and Charles II, the last, in 1651. Moot Hill is now graced by a mausoleum built in the seventeenth century but heavily restored by Atkinson. Precious little survives today of the great Augustinian abbey founded by Alexander I in the 1120s, and whose abbot presided over those king-making ceremonies.

Scotstarvit Tower

near Cupar, Fife
0131 668 8600 | www.historicenvironment.scot

TOWER-HOUSE CASTLE

From the outside, Scotstarvit looks like a typical Jacobean tower house. Inside, though, it has some quirky features. The ground floor is normal enough – a cellar with two narrow window slits, whilst the first floor has two fine windows with stone seats but no fireplace to make it comfortable. The third floor works well as a hall, with a large fireplace, three stone-seated windows, and a privy, as does the fourth floor, also with seated windows and a fireplace, albeit small and stuck at one end. The fifth floor has a fireplace but no windows! The sixth floor, giving access to the wallhead, once had a fireplace, which may solve the riddle. It was taken out and re-erected in the nearby mansion, Hill of Tarvit, where it remains. Dated 1627, it bears the initials SJS and DAD –for Sir John Scot and Dame Anne Drummond, his wife. Sir John was a respectable lawyer when he purchased Inglis Tarvit in 1611. However, in his private life he was regarded as being mildly eccentric. In his dotage he wrote his memorably-titled The Staggering State of the Scots Statesman, which Thomas Carlyle described as 'a strange little book ... a homily on life's nothingness'. Perhaps he wrote it in that fifth-floor room!

Skipness Castle

near Tarbert, Kintyre peninsula, Argyll
0131 668 8600 | www.historicenvironment.scot

ENCLOSURE CASTLE / TOWER-HOUSE CASTLE ■

Three castles in one. It began in the early thirteenth
century as a modest hall-castle with a chapel beside it,
built by Suibhne (Sven) 'the Red'. When the MacSweens
were dispossessed after Norway ceded the Hebrides to
Scotland in 1266, the MacDonald Lord of the Isles built
most of what we now see – a formidable rectangular
castle of enclosure bristling with arrowslits (see right).
After their downfall in 1493, along came the Campbells
to add the lofty tower house (left).

Smailholm Tower

Smailholm, near Kelso, Scottish Borders
01573 460365 | www.historicenvironment.scot

TOWER-HOUSE CASTLE ■

One of the most evocative sights in the Border country.
A lofty, rectangular tower dominating its craig and the
little millpond below. In its shadow the foundations of
an outer feasting hall and kitchen, discovered in 1979.
The Pringles built it in the fifteenth century, but sold out
to the Scotts in 1645. In the 1770s, young Walter Scott
lived nearby and the sight of his ancestors' tower fired
his imagination. The tower now houses an exhibition on
Scott and his Minstrelsy of the Scottish Border.

Spynie Palace

near Elgin, Moray
01343 546358 | www.historicenvironment.scot

HALL CASTLE / TOWER-HOUSE CASTLE

The most complete medieval bishops' residence surviving in Scotland. Home of the Bishops of Moray from the thirteenth century until after the Protestant Reformation in 1560. The substantial ruins of the curtain-walled castle are now dominated by David's Tower, named after its builder, Bishop David Stewart (1462–76). The massive rectangular structure (pictured here), six storeys high, is the largest tower house by volume ever built in Scotland. A spacious great hall and elaborate entrance gateway were added shortly after. Mary Queen of Scots's third husband, the Earl of Bothwell, fled here in 1567, following her surrender at Carberry, near Edinburgh; his uncle Patrick Hepburn was then Bishop of Moray. James Ramsay MacDonald, Labour's first Prime Minister, is buried in the graveyard of nearby Spynie Kirk, once the site of the old cathedral before it was moved to Elgin.

Stirling Castle

Stirling
01786 450000 | www.historicenvironment.scot

ENCLOSURE CASTLE / PALACE

Perhaps Scotland's greatest surviving royal castle, with a recorded history reaching back to Alexander I's reign (1107–24) and associated with such great figures from Scotland's past as William Wallace, Robert the Bruce, and Mary Queen of Scots. Bruce destroyed the castle after his victory over Edward II of England at nearby Bannockburn in 1314, and the oldest part dates only from the 1390s. But it is the buildings created by the royals in the later Middle Ages that are now the highlights – James IV's monumental Great Hall of 1503, James V's sumptuous Palace of c.1540, and James VI's Chapel Royal of 1594. Mary Queen of Scots was crowned here in 1543 and James VI baptized here in 1566. During the Jacobite Risings of the early eighteenth century, new and formidable artillery defences were added, which successfully held out against Bonnie Prince Charlie's army in 1746. The royal stronghold served as the regimental depot of the famous Argyll & Sutherland Highlanders between 1880 and 1964.

Stobo Castle

Stobo, near Peebles, Scottish Borders
01721 725300 | www.stobocastle.co.uk

CASTELLATED MANSION

Once a peaceful 'retreat' for the archbishops of Glasgow,
and now a luxury hotel and spa. Not that anything remains
of their graces' palace, though the nearby twelfth-century
Stobo Kirk, dedicated to St Mungo, Glasgow's patron saint,
is well worth visiting too. The present 'castle' was built
for the Montgomerys in the early nineteenth century,
and subsequently added to.

Stranraer Castle (St John)

Stranraer, Dumfries & Galloway
01776 705088 | www.dumgal.gov.uk

TOWER-HOUSE CASTLE

Also known as the Castle of St John, for reasons unknown.
The L-plan tower house was probably built for the Adairs
of Kilhilt, c.1510, before passing to the Kennedys of
Chapel and then the Dalrymples of Stair. In the early
nineteenth century it was converted into the town jail,
and most of the interior layout and detail dates from
that time, including the prisoners' exercise yard high up
on the roof.

Strome Castle

near Lochcarron, west coast of the Highlands
www.nts.org.uk

TOWER-HOUSE CASTLE

Little remains standing of Strome, precariously perched on a rock overlooking Loch Carron. The location may be of some antiquity, for many west Highland castles have remains reaching back into the Iron Age and beyond; their 'dun' (meaning fort) place names generally give the game away. Not so Strome. Nothing is known of the place until it comes on record in 1472, when Alan Macildny, chief of Clan Cameron, is appointed its constable by Celestine MacDonald, Lord of Lochalsh, and brother of John MacDonald, Lord of the Isles and Earl of Ross. It was besieged and taken in 1503 by the Gordon Earls of Huntly, who from their base at Urquhart, in the Great Glen, had been tasked by James IV to root out lingering support for the newly-deposed Lords of the Isles. Passing by descent to the MacDonells of Glengarry in 1539, the last blow, literally, came in 1602 when Kenneth Mackenzie, 1st Lord Mackenzie of Kintail, besieged the place. With the assistance of Clan Matheson, he succeeded in capturing it, then blowing the place to smithereens. All that remains standing today is a door through the ruined enclosure wall.

Tantallon Castle

near North Berwick, East Lothian
01620 892727 | www.historicenvironment.scot

ENCLOSURE CASTLE

Tantallon was the last great curtain-walled castle constructed in Scotland. Sited high on a cliff overlooking the North Sea, the awesome red sandstone frontal wall was built by William, 1st Earl of Douglas, c.1360. It still stands virtually complete, together with its three great projecting towers. In the 1380s, the House of Douglas split into two, the 'Black' and 'Red', and Tantallon passed to the latter, who became Earls of Angus. They held sway from here for another 300 years. Tantallon was built in an age before gunpowdered artillery posed a threat. Nevertheless, it resisted two fully-pressed royal sieges, by James IV in 1491 and James V in 1528. The latter, however, caused extensive damage, and repairs subsequently carried out, using a local green stone, are obvious today. In its twilight days the Earls built a two-storey house in the courtyard (right) to replace the immensely high Douglas Tower behind (centre). The final siege, by Cromwell's forces in 1651, wrought such devastation that the Douglases had to abandon their mighty medieval fortress to the birds.

Tarbert Castle

Tarbert, Kintyre peninsula, Argyll
www.tarbertcastle.info

ENCLOSURE CASTLE

Robert the Bruce spent most of his reign (1306–29) demolishing castles, to prevent them being of use to the enemy, the English. Tarbert is the sole exception. Strategically sited overlooking Tarbert harbour, it controlled movement across the narrow isthmus linking East and West Loch Tarbert, a passage made famous c.1098 when King Magnus Barelegs of Norway had his longship dragged over it to symbolize his possession of the Hebrides. Quite what sense we make of the ivy-clad ruins and turf-covered walls will have to await excavation. We know that Bruce's castle, built to house his new sheriff of Argyll, included stone buildings as well as timber and clay structures, and there is clear evidence for a large enclosure castle. More clear is the date of the oblong tower that today dominates the spot. This was built by James IV in 1494, as part of his campaign to overthrow the over-mighty MacDonalds, Lords of the Isles.

Taymouth Castle

Kenmore, Perth & Kinross
01887 830226 | www.taymouth-castle.com

CASTELLATED MANSION

Known in the seventeenth century as Balloch, when
Sir Duncan Campbell of Glenorchy, 'Black Duncan of
the Castles', relocated from his Argyllshire seat at
Kilchurn in the 1620s. Nothing survives of his large
Z-plan tower house, for all was swept away when the
present sprawling mansion was built 1801–42 by John
Campbell and his son, respectively 1st and 2nd Earl of
Breadalbane. By the 1920s the Campbells had gone,
and the vast complex took on its new role as a hotel.

Thirlestane Castle

Lauder, Scottish Borders
01578 722430 | www.thirlestanecastle.co.uk

TOWER-HOUSE CASTLE

One of Scotland's finest castles. Built originally by Sir John Maitland, James VI's chancellor, in the late sixteenth century, his impressive tower house was superbly remodelled a century later by his namesake, the Duke of Lauderdale, Charles II's Secretary for Scotland. His architects were Sir William Bruce and Robert Mylne, fresh from redesigning the Palace of Holyroodhouse for His Majesty. The castle sits on an artillery fort built by the English in the 1540s, which in turn sits on a twelfth-century motte-and-bailey.

Threave Castle

near Castle Douglas, Dumfries & Galloway
07711 223101 | www.historicenvironment.scot

TOWER-HOUSE CASTLE

Legendary stronghold of the ancient Lords of Galloway.
Today dominated by the forbidding tower built by Archibald
'the Grim', 3rd Earl of Douglas, c.1370. Among the first
of its kind built in Scotland, with an entrance at first-
floor level and battlements fitted with a unique fighting
gallery. 'The Grim' died here in 1400. In 1455, the
over-mighty Black Douglases, preparing for a 'showdown'
with James II, built an innovative artillery work around
the tower. It worked, for the king had to bribe its garrison
into surrender.

Tolquhon Castle

near Pitmedden, Aberdeenshire
01651 851286 | www.historicenvironment.scot

TOWER-HOUSE CASTLE

Arguably Aberdeenshire's most picturesque castle.
Chiefly the work of one man, William Forbes, 7th laird
of Tolquhon, who built everything bar the early fifteenth-
century 'auld tour' (left) in 1584–89. His splendid new
home, a three-storeyed residential block at the far end
of a courtyard, is entered through the twin-towered
gatehouse – a real gem, designed to impress not deter
the visitor. It still does, as does the 'glorious tomb' he
erected for him and his wife in nearby Tarves kirkyard.

Traquair House

Innerleithen, near Peebles, Scottish Borders
01896 830323 | www.traquair.co.uk

TOWER-HOUSE CASTLE ✳ ◼

Said to be the oldest continuously inhabited house in
Scotland, although nothing earlier than the early
sixteenth century has yet to be detected. The history of
the site certainly goes back to the twelfth century, when
the kings built a hunting lodge beside the confluence of
the Quair Water and the River Tweed. The oldest part of
the present building is a tower house at the north end
(left), probably erected by James Stewart, son of the Earl
of Buchan, who acquired the lands in 1491. Sir James
founded the line that became Earls of Traquair in 1633.
During that time, the tower house was altered and
added to, appearing today much as it would have done
c.1642 when the 1st Earl regularized the fenestration to
make it look all of a piece. In the 1690s the 4th Earl had
two low courtyard ranges added (far left and far right).
The most important addition since then has to be the
famous Bear Gates (not those pictured), erected by the
5th Earl at the main entrance to the grounds in the 1730s.
The story goes that after Bonnie Prince Charlie left here
for England in 1745, the Earl locked the gates, vowing
they would never be opened until a Stewart sat on the
throne once more. They remain padlocked to this day.

Urquhart Castle

Drumnadrochit, near Inverness
01456 450551 | www.historicenvironment.scot

ENCLOSURE CASTLE / TOWER-HOUSE CASTLE

Urquhart's history goes back to the Dark Ages. St Columba visited c.580, baptizing a Pictish nobleman in his fort here. The English captured the castle in 1296 only for the Scots to retake it soon after. In the later Middle Ages, the MacDonald Lords of the Isles ruled from here. After their overthrow in 1493, James IV gave it to the Grants of Freuchie, who rebuilt the castle with a twin-towered gatehouse and the Grant Tower overlooking the loch. In 1692 Redcoats blew the gatehouse up to prevent the castle falling into Jacobite hands.

Index

Where to look for more information

The Gazetteer for Scotland is a vast online encyclopedia, featuring details of towns, villages, bens, and glens from the Scottish Borders to the Northern Isles. It includes tourist attractions, industries, and historic sites, together with histories of family names and biographies of famous people associated with Scotland.
Website www.scottish-places.info

Historic Scotland properties are managed by Historic Environment Scotland who have responsibility for maintaining and promoting more than 300 properties of national importance. Historic Environment Scotland was formed in 2015 from the merger of the government agency Historic Scotland and the Royal Commission on the Ancient and Historical Monuments of Scotland (RCAHMS).
Telephone 0131 668 8600;
Website www.historicenvironment.scot

Historic Environment Scotland also maintain Canmore, an online database which was previously maintained by Royal Commission on the Ancient and Historical Monuments of Scotland. The Canmore database is a part of the National Monuments Record of Scotland (NMRS) and provides access to a great wealth of information and

material on the sites, monuments, and buildings of Scotland's past.
Telephone 0131 662 1456; Website canmore.org.uk

Scran is an online history and culture resource service with over 360 000 images to search, collect, and use. Resources range from castles to capercaillies, and from Greyfriar's Bobby to Gregory's Girl. It is designed for both lifelong learning and formal education. Anyone may search the contents and view thumbnails for free. Additional services are supplied under subscription.
Telephone 0131 662 1211; e-mail scran@scran.ac.uk; website www.scran.ac.uk

The National Trust for Scotland is Scotland's leading conservation organisation. It is not a government department, but a charity supported by its membership of almost a quarter of a million people. The Trust was founded in 1931 by a small group of Scots concerned at the growing threat to the country's natural and built heritage. Now, it is an influential body with more than a hundred diverse properties. Its remit, set out in various Acts of Parliament, is to promote the care and conservation of the Scottish landscape and historic buildings while providing access for the public to enjoy them.
Telephone 0844 493 2100; e-mail information@nts.org.uk; website www.nts.org.uk

VisitScotland is Scotland's national tourist authority and can provide information on any aspect of a visit to Scotland. Telephone: 0845 859 1006; e-mail info@visitscotland.com; website www.visitscotland.com

Further reading

Martin Coventry *The Castles of Scotland* (5th edition, Musselburgh, 2015)
A comprehensive reference and gazetteer to over 2000 castles.

Stewart Cruden *The Scottish Castle* (3rd edition, London, 1981)
The standard textbook for students.

John Dunbar *Scottish Royal Palaces* (Edinburgh, 1999)
All you need to know about their building, and their use as royal residences.

Charles McKean *The Scottish Chateau* (Stroud, 2004)

Chris Tabraham *Scotland's Castles* (2nd edition, London, 2005)
An exploration of the Scottish castle and the people who built and lived in them.

Books for children

Richard Dargie *Scottish Castles through History* (Wayland, 1998)
Richard Dargie *Medieval Scotland* (Heinemann, 2002)

Photo credits

Collins

LITTLE BOOKS

These beautifully presented Little Books make excellent pocket-sized guides, packed with hints and tips.

Bananagrams Secrets
978-0-00-825046-1
£6.99

Bridge Secrets
978-0-00-825047-8
£6.99

101 ways to win at Scrabble
978-0-00-758914-2
£6.99

Gin
978-0-00-825810-8
£6.99

PUBLISHERS

Since 1817